# IQ
# CHALLENGE

# IQ
# CHALLENGE

**BARNES & NOBLE**

NEW YORK

Puzzles created by Keith Charlton and Tamara Green except:
Puzzles on pages 36, 62 (b), 69 (b), 156 (b), 157 (t), 164 (t), 170, 171 (t), 174 (b), 188
© 2004 Puzzle Media Ltd

Design by Marilyn Franks

ISBN-13: 978-0-7607-5956-1
ISBN-10: 0-7607-5956-1

Printed and bound in China

3   5   7   9   10   8   6   4

# Contents

# Introduction

**How intelligent are you? Can you think logically as well as laterally? Have you lots of staying power? You are about to find out, as you begin to tackle the wide range of puzzles in *IQ Challenge*.**

The conundrums and brain teasers in this book – some visual, some verbal, some numerical – have been divided into 20 sections according to level of complexity in the main. Some types of puzzle, you will also find, are repeated at intervals, so you should be able to solve them all the more speedily with practice. Indeed, any that appear difficult to start with may soon become walk-overs as you learn to master the sort of approach needed.

No specific time limits have been set for each section, but you might like to introduce these yourself. See how long it takes you to complete Level 1, for instance; and then aim to finish Level 2 in the same time, or maybe less.

All the answers are printed at the back of the book. In most instances, you will also find an explanation. You may at times be tempted to look at them but it is worthwhile resisting unless you are well and truly stumped. Instead, give a little more time and thought to the puzzle you are attempting and you may suddenly see the light for yourself.

Above all, though, don't get bogged down. Puzzle-solving is not only an excellent way of sharpening your wits, it is also meant to be fun. So by the time you have completed the very last challenge on page 194 (a code that includes a special message for everyone buying this book), you should not only have spent many enjoyable hours, but your brain will undoubtedly have benefited, too. In fact, once you get started, you may well become so fascinated that it will be hard to put this volume down. Try it and see!

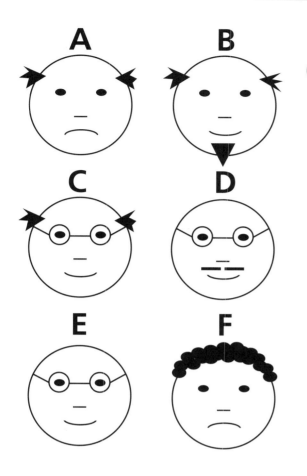

**A**      **B**

**C**      **D**

**E**      **F**

**1** From the following descriptions, can you work out who's who?

**John** wears glasses and is bald.

**Max** always looks miserable.

**Gavin** has a beard.

**Sid** has a moustache.

**Eric** has a receding hairline.

**Paul** has a good head of hair.

**2** What number should replace the question mark?

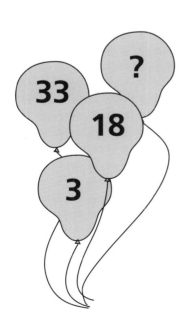

**3** Can you rearrange the blocks below to form a magic square? Each horizontal row, vertical column and diagonal line must add up to 24.

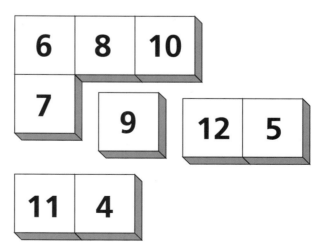

**4** Joshua was famed throughout the land as court jester, his jokes keeping the royal family amused for hours on end. His reputation slipped, however, after he accidentally hit the king on the head with a wayward club which was one of the four he was attempting to keep airborne. When, at last, his lord and master had regained consciousness, Joshua was not at all surprised to be taken away and thrown into a cell in the North Tower as punishment for his clumsiness.

Picking himself out of a heap of straw, Joshua brushed himself down and tried to regain some self-composure. Surprise! Surprise! On looking around the cell, he was glad to see the familiar face of his old friend, Max the Magician. (Max had been thrown into gaol three months earlier after one of *his* tricks had gone wrong, too, and the king's hair had turned bright red.)

Max laughed when Joshua told him why he had been incarcerated, saying that it served the king right for being such a moody knave.

Pleasantries aside, Joshua now began to explore the cell. The walls were solid and damp; but to his surprise, the window had no bars. On looking through the opening, he could see why; the drop was so deep, it would be suicidal to attempt an escape. "What I really need is a rope," Joshua said forlornly.

Immediately, Max produced a thick, plaited rope from the sleeve of his cloak. "Will this do?" he asked. But the rope was far too short, reaching only halfway down. It would still be too dangerous to drop the remaining distance.

"Don't worry, old friend," Max continued, "I'll get you safely to the ground. There's a simple solution and it doesn't even require any magic. As for me, I think I'll stay here. I'm old now, and I like an easy life."

**How did Max succeed in getting Joshua to the ground?**

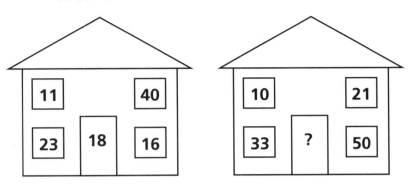

**5** What number is missing from the second front door?

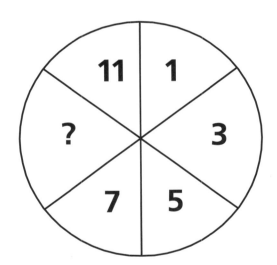

**6** What number replaces the question mark?

**7** Three men – Mr Baker, Mr Joiner and Mr Driver – are a baker, a joiner and a driver, but their surnames do not necessarily correspond to their jobs. The driver, in any event, is not Mr Baker, nor does Mr Driver's name match his job; and the man who is the baker has a name that does not correspond to Mr Joiner's occupation.

What is Mr Driver's occupation?

9

**8** Can you use the table below to find the name of a composer?

| 1 | 2 | 3 | 4 | 5 | 6 | 7 | 8 | 9 | 10 | 11 | 12 | 13 |
|---|---|---|---|---|---|---|---|---|----|----|----|----|
| A | B | C | D | E | F | G | H | I | J | K | L | M |
| N | O | P | Q | R | S | T | U | V | W | X | Y | Z |

| 6 | 3 | 8 | 8 | 13 | 1 | 1 | 1 |
|---|---|---|---|----|---|---|---|
|   |   |   |   |    |   |   |   |

**9** Which number should replace the question mark?

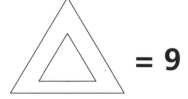

△ = 9

□ = 16

⬠ = ?

| A | L | K | J |
|---|---|---|---|
| B | M | ? | I |
| C | N | O | H |
| D | E | F | G |

**10** Which letter completes this grid and why?

**11** At a dinner party, Bob, Colin, David, Emily, Frances and Georgina are to be seated at a circular table. Strangely, no two of them whose initials are next to each other in the alphabet will sit side by side.

If Colin is to be seated opposite Frances, can you draw a possible table plan?

**12** Can you put these heads in a logical order?

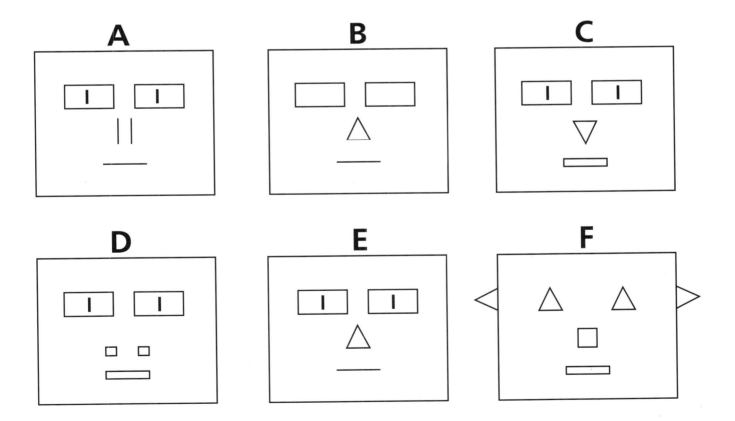

**13** What regular shape can be formed by arranging the four pieces below?

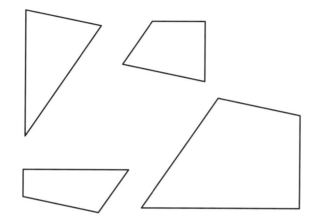

**15** On which square must you start in order to cross every square?

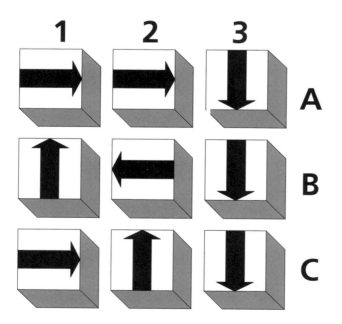

**14** Marilyn has been trying to give up smoking, and a friend has suggested that she does not try to stop 'cold turkey' but should give up gradually. If she cuts down by 20 per cent for the first week, her friend has explained, a further 25 per cent of the amount she is then smoking for the second week, and 50 per cent of the number she is then smoking for the third week, she will only be smoking 3 per day at that stage.

**How many cigarettes is Marilyn currently smoking per day?**

**16** Can you unscramble the letters to reveal two sports?

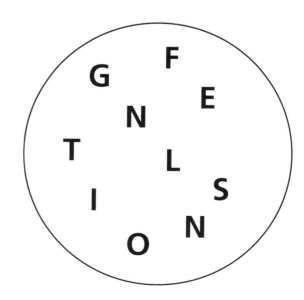

**17** What number replaces the question mark?

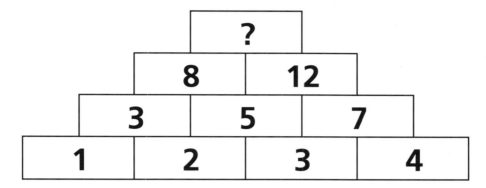

**18** Can you work out which letter comes next?

# OTTFFS?

**19** What card comes next in the series?

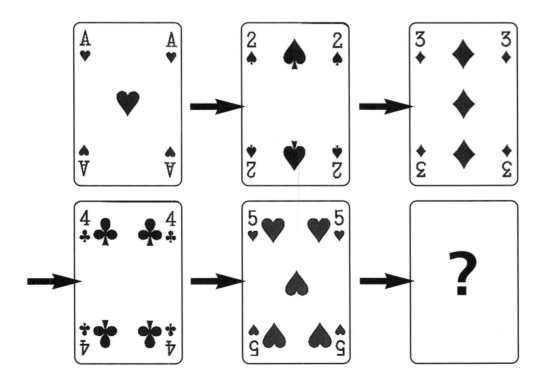

**20** Can you put the correct mathematical symbols into the spaces to make the sum accurate?

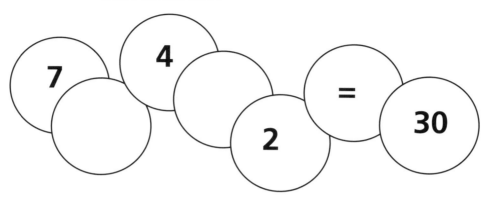

**21** Can you use the logic of the first diagram to complete the second figure?

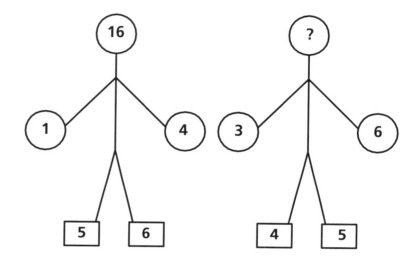

**22** This Christmas, **Anna** will not get a scarf unless **Mary** gets perfume.
**Anna** will not get chocolates unless **Sarah** gets the scarf.
**Anna** will not get the perfume unless Mary gets the chocolates.
**Sarah** will not get a scarf unless **Anna** gets the perfume; and **Mary** will not get the chocolates unless **Sarah** gets the perfume.

**Can you work out which present each will receive?**

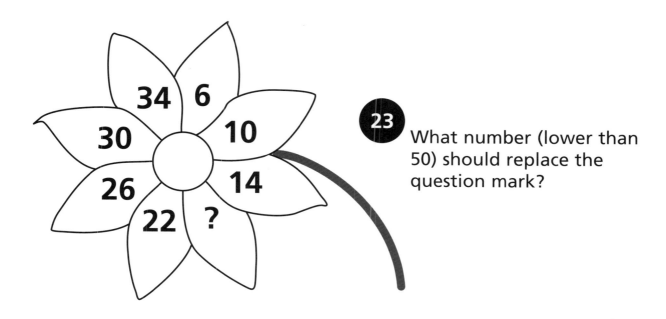

**23** What number (lower than 50) should replace the question mark?

**24** Which letter lies two letters below the letter which is one place to the right of **B**?

| B | D | C |
|---|---|---|
| H | A | F |
| G | E | I |

**25** Can you rearrange these boxes to form three nine-letter words?

| TIC | ORB | EST |
|-----|-----|-----|
| BAS | ISH | ABL |
| BOM | ENT | ABS |

**26** Which shape completes the grid shown – **1**, **2** or **3**?

| B | D | A | C | E |
|---|---|---|---|---|
| C | E |   | D | A |
| D |   |   |   | B |
| E | B |   | A | C |
| A | C | E | B | D |

**1**

|   | B |   |
|---|---|---|
| A | C | E |
|   | D |   |

**2**

|   | B |   |
|---|---|---|
| A | E | C |
|   | D |   |

**3**

|   | D |   |
|---|---|---|
| E | C | A |
|   | B |   |

**27** Which shape fits the hole – **A**, **B** or **C**?

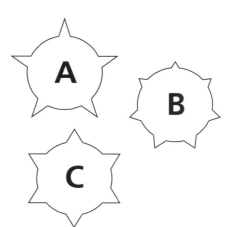

# LEVEL 2

**1** Can you assign numerical values (all whole numbers lower than 10) to the shapes △, ○ and □ below so that the see-saws are perfectly balanced? You should then be able to work out what replaces the question mark – **A**, **B** or **C**.

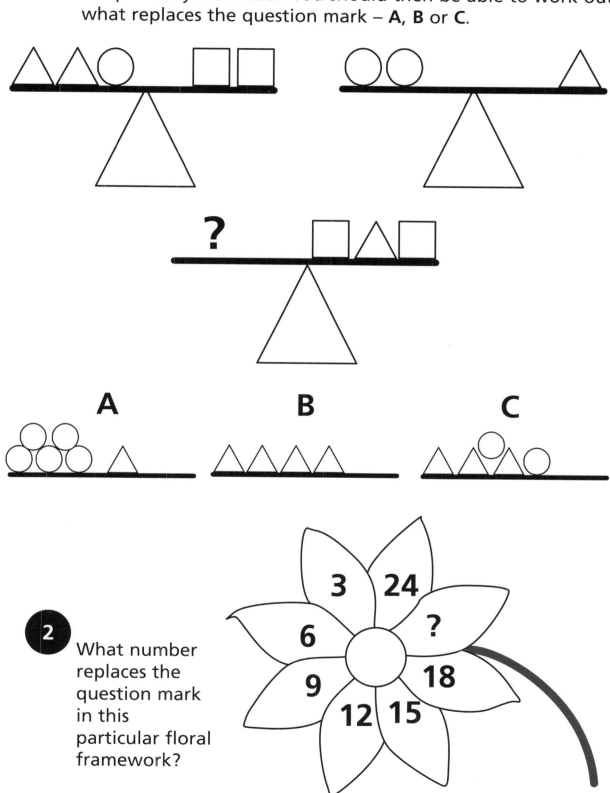

**A**

**B**

**C**

**2** What number replaces the question mark in this particular floral framework?

3  24  6  ?  9  18  12  15

**3** Which shape should replace the question mark?

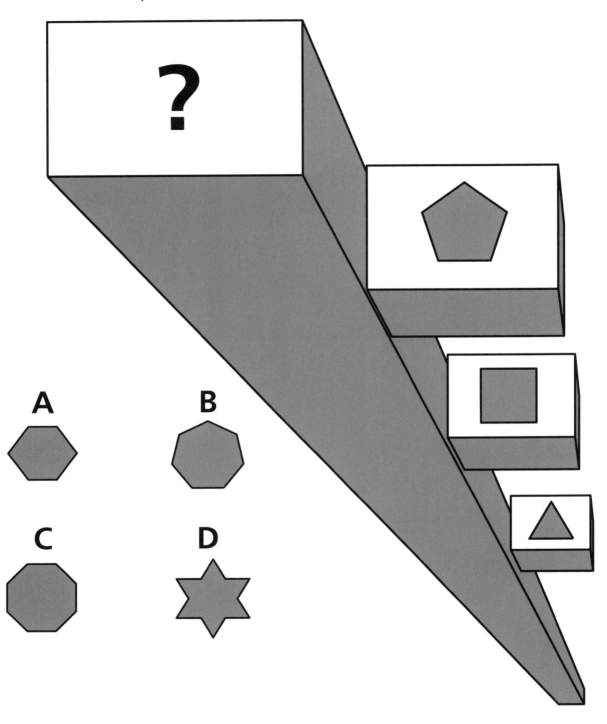

**A**

**B**

**C**

**D**

**4** Can you make 5 equilateral triangles using 9 matches?

**5** What regular shape can be formed by the four shapes shown here, if they are joined together?

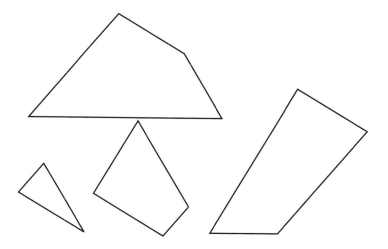

**6** Can you find four different numbers totalling 54, so that:
if you add 2 to one of the numbers,
if you take 2 from another number,
if you multiply the third number by 2, AND
if you divide the fourth number by 2,
the answer will always be the same?

**7** At a crowded gathering, Nancy recalled having been introduced to a tall, rather handsome guy but could not remember the next day how he was related to Annabel who had introduced them, although she did remember that his name was Justin.

When chatting over the telephone, Annabel – more than a little put out to be asked these questions because she knew that Nancy could be very flirtatious, particularly with blonde young men – decided to give a cryptic reply.

She explained that Justin's mother was in fact *her* mother's only surviving child.

**Can you tell from the information provided how Annabel was actually related to Justin?**

**8** Can you use the logic of the first diagram to complete the second figure?

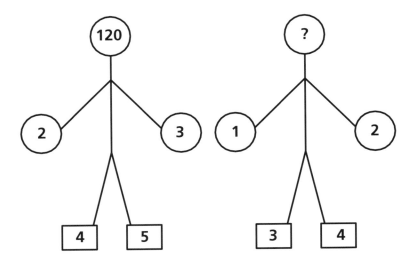

**9** Can you spot the odd one out?

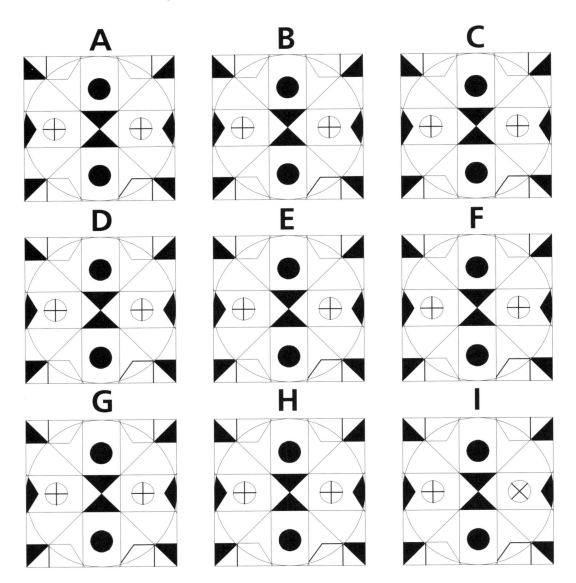

A  B  C

D  E  F

G  H  I

**10** What symbols should replace the question mark?

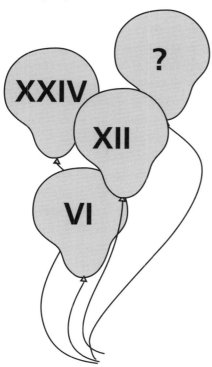

**XXIV**

**XII**

**?**

**VI**

|  | A | B | C |
|---|---|---|---|
| 1 | ↓ | ← | ← |
| 2 | ↓ | ↓ | ↑ |
| 3 | → | → | ↑ |

**11** On which square must you start in the above puzzle in order to cross every square?

**12** Which shape fits the hole – **A**, **B** or **C**?

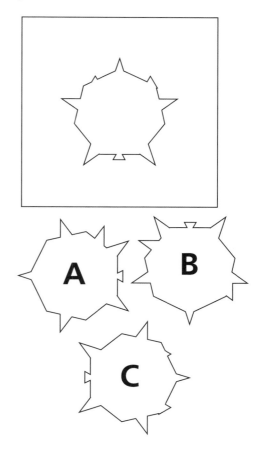

**13** What number should replace the question mark?

7 — 4    ?

3   10

4   5   12

7 — 5

5 — 7 — 3

**14** Can you use the table below to find the name of a mythical monster?

| 1 | 2 | 3 | 4 | 5 | 6 | 7 | 8 | 9 | 10 | 11 | 12 | 13 |
|---|---|---|---|---|---|---|---|---|----|----|----|----|
| A | B | C | D | E | F | G | H | I | J  | K  | L  | M  |
| N | O | P | Q | R | S | T | U | V | W  | X  | Y  | Z  |

| 13 | 5 | 4 | 8 | 6 | 1 |
|----|---|---|---|---|---|
|    |   |   |   |   |   |

**15** What number should replace the question mark?

8
9    8

12
7    6

?
5    9

**16** In the Marsh family, each girl has twice as many brothers as she has sisters. However, each boy has the same number of brothers as sisters. Is this possible; and, if so, how many girls are there in the family, and how many boys?

**17** What card comes next in the series?

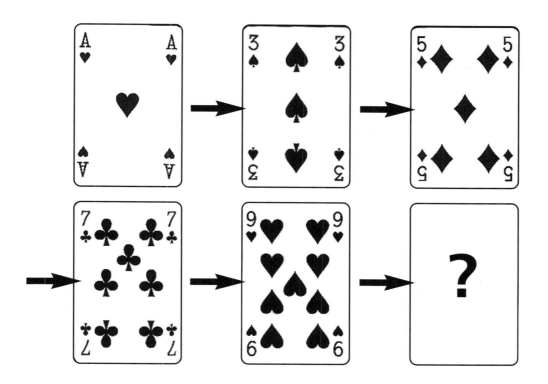

**18** Can you put the correct mathematical symbols into the blank spaces to make the sum correct?

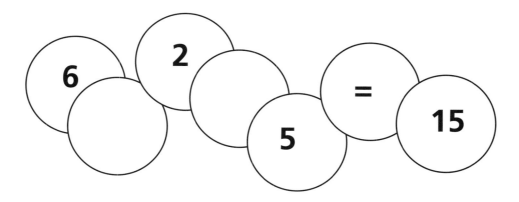

**19** What is the next letter in the series?

# MTWTFS?

**20** Whilst he was alive, Lord Baffle had always enjoyed testing his two sons, Billy and Bobby, with all manner of riddles and tests of ingenuity. (He had hoped to improve their minds and make them independent, but instead they only grew lazy, and insolent to boot). Upon his death, his sons thought all this would end, but they were in for an unpleasant surprise.

On the day of the reading of the will, all of Lord Baffle's beneficiaries gathered in the Great Hall of the family mansion. Each in turn received sums of money or family heirlooms, until finally it was the turn of Billy and Bobby.

"To my sons." Mr Grabbit, the solicitor, read from the will, "I leave each, one of my two sports cars. These are, as my sons know fine well, identical in every way apart from in colour. I therefore leave the black car to Billy, and the white car to Bobby." Mr Grabbit paused for a moment and then continued: "The rest of my considerable estate I leave to whichever son wins a race between these two cars. The race will take place along the half-mile of the driveway. The rules of the race are a little unusual and will be as follows:
1. The winner of the race shall be the brother whose car crosses the finishing line in *second place*.
2. The race must be a proper race, both brothers having to drive flat out for the finishing line with the *aim* of crossing it *before* the other.
3. If the brothers cannot work out how to meet these criteria within three days of the reading of this document, Mr Grabbit is advised that I am happy to leave the remaining estate to the Inland Revenue."

The brothers looked at each other in horror. At last their father had got his way: they were going to have to use their brains and work for their inheritance!

**How did the brothers fulfil their father's wishes and save the rest of the estate from going to the tax man?**

**21** Can you fill the empty box?

| 2 | 9 | 7 |
|---|---|---|
| 3 | 11 | 8 |
| 5 | 7 | |
| 4 | 10 | 6 |

**22** Can you rearrange the groups of letters in these boxes to form three nine-letter words?

| ART | ILI | RKS |
|-----|-----|-----|
| LMA | HAL | ARY |
| IAL | AUX | IMP |

**1** First arrange 16 matches as in the figure shown.
Can you now move only three matches to a different position to make just four squares?

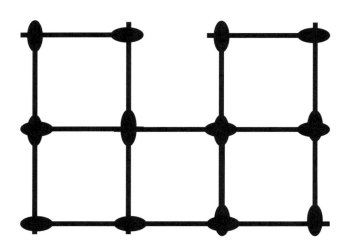

**2** What letters replace the question marks?

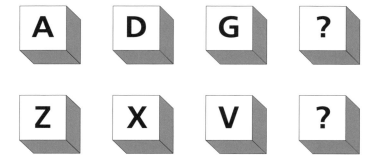

**3** John likes to gamble, and his latest wheeze is to tell everyone at a party that he bets at least two people in the room were born in the same season – spring, summer, autumn or winter. But he's canny.
He knows he will only win the bet if there are at least a certain number of people in the room at the time.
How many people should be present if John is definitely to go home a richer man?

**4** Can you set out the numbers 1-9 around this triangle by the side of the spots shown so that the total of the numbers on each side of the triangle comes to 17?

**5** Alice, Susan, David and Steven all loved to visit their Great Aunt Bess. She always had some new game to play, or puzzle for them to solve, and today was no exception.

After their usual snack of lemonade and rock buns, Aunt Bess sat the four children down at the kitchen table. She then got out a pack of playing cards which she divided into the four suits, and handed one suit to each child. She next took a suit of cards from another pack and proceeded to deal them on to the table as follows:

1. She turned the top card over and placed it on the table.
2. She moved the new top card to the bottom of the pack.
3. She turned the new top card over and placed it on the table.
4. She moved the new top card to the bottom of the pack.
5. She continued the above steps until only one card remained. Then she turned it over and placed it on the table next to the others.

When Aunt Bess had finished dealing her cards, the children were amused to see that all the cards had been placed on the table in order, from ace through to king. The problem she set the children was to arrange their cards in such a way as to be able to duplicate her performance.

**In what order should the children have arranged their cards?**

**6** On which square must you start in order to cover every square?

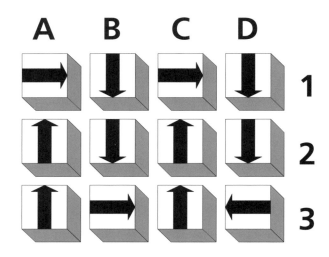

A   B   C   D

**7** What number will complete this grid?

| 3 | 1 | 7 | ? |
|---|---|---|---|
| 6 | 10 | 4 | 1 |
| 3 | 9 | 7 | 2 |

**8** Put out 7 coins in a circle and make sure they are all heads-up. Now pick any coin and, going in a clockwise direction, move past two coins and turn over the third, so that it is tails-up.

Keep doing this, each time starting with any coin that is still heads-up and ignoring any that are now tails up. Your aim is to turn over all the coins so that they are tails-up, except for one.

**9** Can you use the logic of the first diagram to complete the second one?

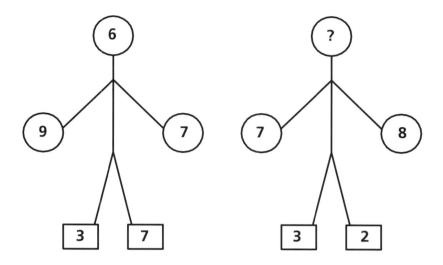

**10** What figure should replace the question mark in the circle below?

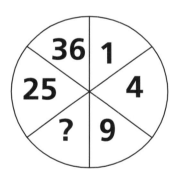

**11** What number should be inserted in the third triangle?

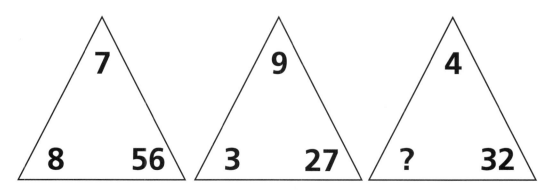

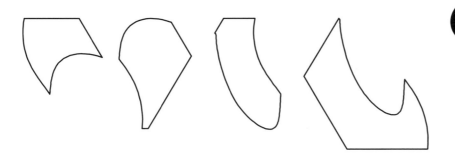

**12** What regular shape can you form by arranging the four pieces left?

**13** Can you spot the odd one out?

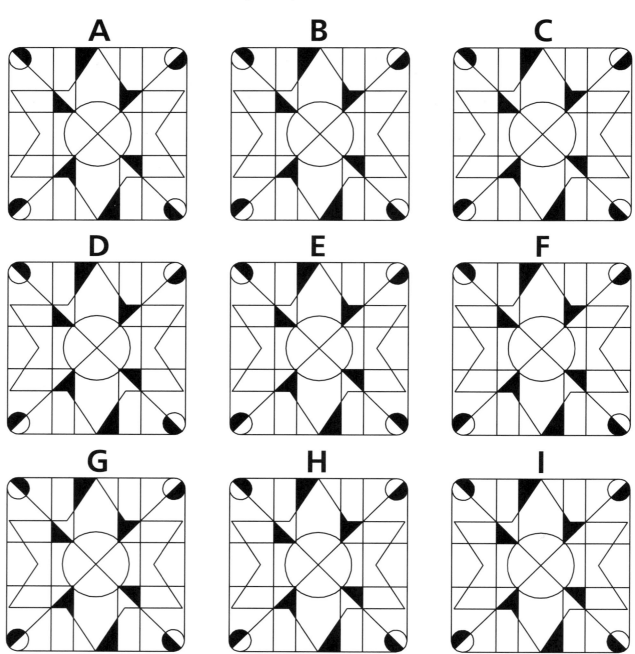

**A**  **B**  **C**

**D**  **E**  **F**

**G**  **H**  **I**

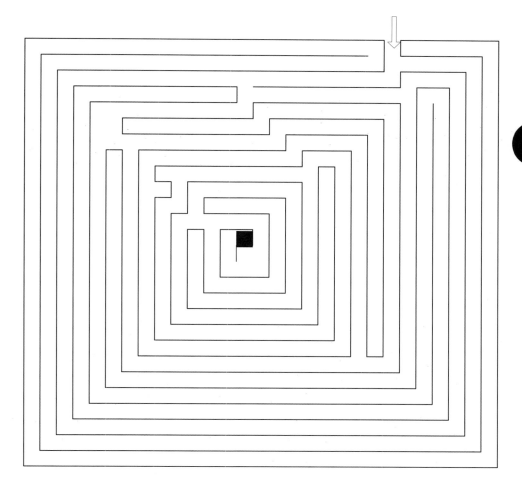

**14** Which is the most direct route to the centre of this maze?

**15** Which letter is one below the letter which is just to the left of the letter which is just above the letter which lies between D and P?

| G | R | M |
|---|---|---|
| D | O | P |
| L | N | Q |

**16** What number comes next in this series?

312 — 267 — 222 — 177 — ?

**17** Can you use the table below to find the name of a famous actor?

| 1 | 2 | 3 | 4 | 5 | 6 | 7 | 8 | 9 | 10 | 11 | 12 | 13 |
|---|---|---|---|---|---|---|---|---|----|----|----|----|
| A | B | C | D | E | F | G | H | I | J | K | L | M |
| N | O | P | Q | R | S | T | U | V | W | X | Y | Z |

| 5 | 9 | 3 | 8 | 1 | 5 | 4 |
|---|---|---|---|---|---|---|
|   |   |   |   |   |   |   |

| 2 | 8 | 5 | 7 | 2 | 1 |
|---|---|---|---|---|---|
|   |   |   |   |   |   |

**18** In John Hinde's will, he left $68,000 in total – to his three brothers and their wives, Annie, Barbara and Sue. But he did not leave equal amounts to each beneficiary.
Annie was to receive $5,000 more than Barbara, who inherited the same amount as her husband. Sue received $3,000 more than Steve, and Bill received $6,000 less than his wife who was not Annie. Chris inherited $10,000, which was $1,000 less than Steve.

**Who was married to whom, and how much did each receive?**

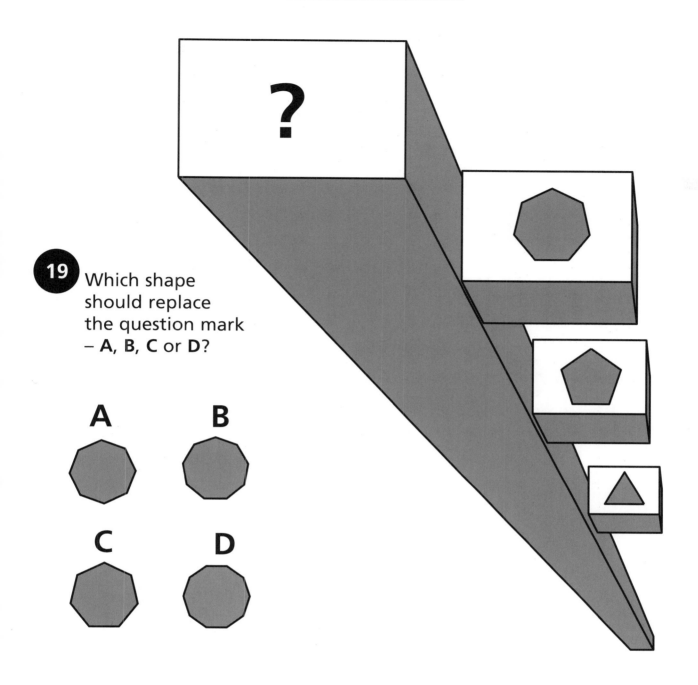

**19** Which shape should replace the question mark – **A**, **B**, **C** or **D**?

A    B

C    D

**20** Can you rearrange these boxes to form three nine-letter words?

| LAN | TOR | BEA |
|-----|-----|-----|
| GAL | FUL | IGA |
| UTI | TRY | NAV |

**21** Which shape fits the hole – **A**, **B**, **C** or **D**?
Any shape may be rotated, but not flipped over.

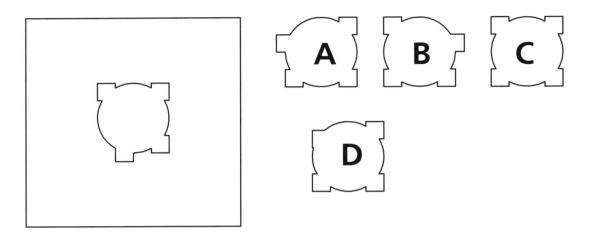

**22** What card comes next in this series?

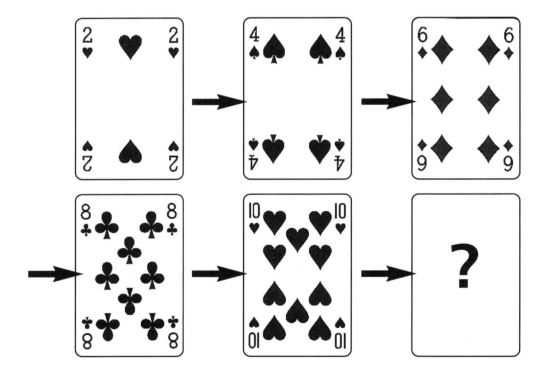

**23** Which letter replaces the question mark?

# JFMAM?

**24** Will and Dill (short for Dylan) had perfected a party piece which involved a thought-reading act. Dill would go out of the room and Will would invite the other guests to decide on a word together. They then had to continue thinking of it so that Dill might read their thoughts while blindfolded, allowing no possibility for visual communication. Will would then start to ask him questions to see if Dill could guess the word in question.

On one particular occasion, for instance, he asked Dill:
"Did we think of the word *sock*?"
"Absolutely not!" replied Dill.
"Well, are we thinking of an *ashtray*?"
"No", replied Dill, with a wry smile.
"Okay. Are we thinking of the word *plate*?"
Again the answer was in the negative.
"So are we thinking of the word *china*?"
"No, no", said Dill again.
"Are we thinking of *carpet*?"
"No", replied Dill, even more confidently this time.
"The word you are thinking of is *chair*!"
Everyone at the party gasped. He was right!

**How had Dill managed to get the correct answer?**

**25** What four-figure number (containing all the same digits) should replace the question mark?

| 8,882 | 9,996 | 1,234 | 9,134 | 7,656 |
| 8,888 | 9,122 | 4,444 | 8,294 | 6,667 |
| 8,221 | 5,541 | 7,366 | 9,992 | 9,688 |
| 2,953 | 4,566 | 1,999 | 9,876 | ? |
| 5,555 | 7,767 | 9,799 | 2,432 | 3,654 |

**1** A standard set of dominoes has been laid out, using numbers instead of dots for clarity. Using a sharp pencil and a keen brain, can you draw in the lines to show where each domino has been placed? You may find the check grid useful – cross off each domino as you find it.

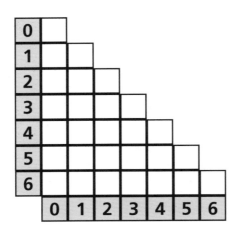

| 2 | 4 | 1 | 5 | 5 | 3 | 1 | 3 |
|---|---|---|---|---|---|---|---|
| 5 | 1 | 4 | 1 | 6 | 0 | 3 | 4 |
| 5 | 0 | 1 | 3 | 2 | 5 | 3 | 5 |
| 3 | 6 | 2 | 6 | 4 | 0 | 0 | 6 |
| 1 | 1 | 2 | 2 | 0 | 0 | 4 | 2 |
| 0 | 2 | 0 | 4 | 6 | 1 | 6 | 4 |
| 5 | 5 | 6 | 3 | 6 | 3 | 2 | 4 |

**2** Can you identify the missing card?

**3** Can you use the logic of the first diagram to complete the one to the right?

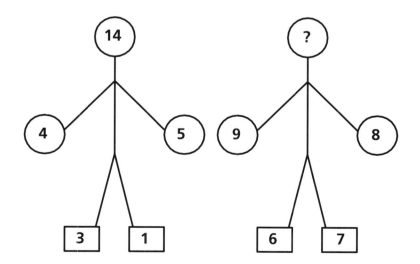

**4** Which letter should replace the question mark?

R

F ?

B D H

**5** Enlarge the diagram and place 9 coins on the central squares.
Make one coin jump over another and remove the one jumped over.
Continue until you have just one coin left centrally in position 5.

**In what order should the jumps proceed?**

| | | | | |
|---|---|---|---|---|
| | | | | |
| | 1 | 2 | 3 | |
| | 4 | 5 | 6 | |
| | 7 | 8 | 9 | |
| | | | | |

**6** One day, Fred Handyman went to the builders' merchants and bought a plank of wood. Then, when he got home, he sawed the plank in half and stained the two halves, ready to be made into shelves.

When his wife asked him how long the shelves would be, Fred told her that each shelf was equal in length to half-a-shelf plus 50cm (20in). His wife, annoyed at such a cryptic answer, promptly walked away in disgust.

**From the information given by Fred, can you work out how short the original plank could have been?**

**7** Can you assign numerical values (all whole numbers lower than 10) to the shapes □, ○ and △ so that the see-saws are perfectly balanced? You should then be able to work out what replaces the question mark – **A**, **B** or **C**.

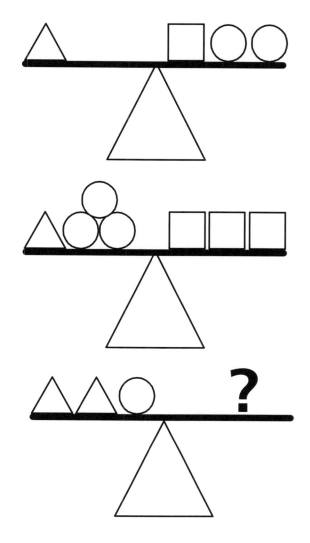

**A**

**B**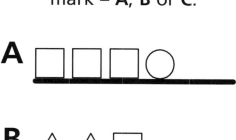

**C**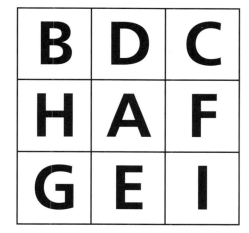

**8** Which letter lies one letter below the letter which is one place to the left of the letter two places above the letter which is two places to the right of G?

| B | D | C |
| H | A | F |
| G | E | I |

**9** What number comes next in the series?

90 — 74 — 66 — 62 — ?

39

**10** Which shape fits the hole – **A**, **B**, **C** or **D**?
Shapes may be rotated but not flipped over.

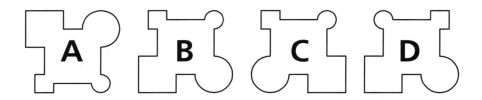

**11** What number should replace the question mark?

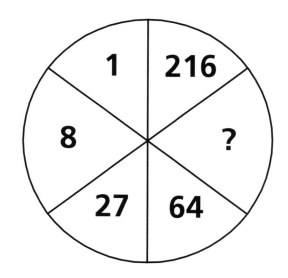

**12** Can you unscramble the letters to reveal two countries?

**13** Professor Matrix was a brilliant mathematician, but he was also slightly absent-minded. When he received a new safe one day, he decided that the best way to remember the combination would be to think of it as a unique calculation. He therefore set his combination to use all of the ten digits, 0-9, but once only. He then thought of the first two digits of the combination as a two-figure number; the next three digits of the combination became a three-figure number in his mind; and this three-figure number was a multiple of the first two-figure number. Finally, he made the last five digits of the combination a five-figure number, and the product of the first two numbers if they were multiplied together.

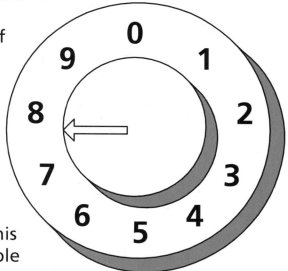

**From this information, can you work out the combination to his safe?**

**14** First arrange 15 matches as shown *below*. Can you then take away 6 to leave 100?

  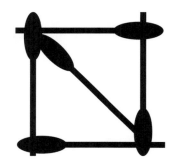

**15** Can you spot the odd one out?

A      B      C

D      E      F

G      H      I

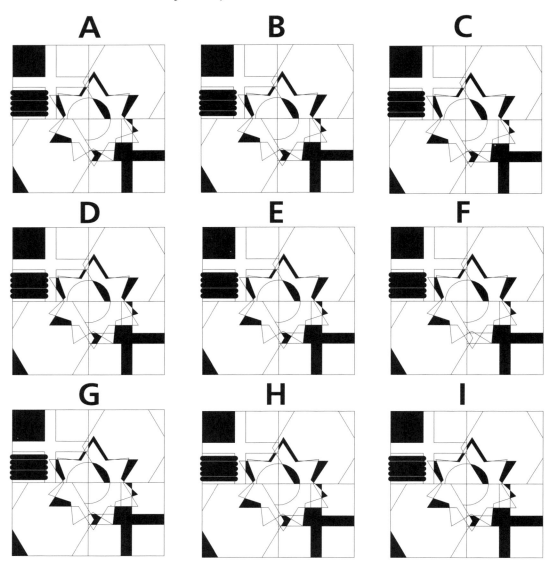

**16** Alice's husband, Freddie, is 4 years older than she is, and twice as old now as she was 17 years ago.

**Can you work out their ages?**

**17** Can you find the odd man out?

run

jump

sit

slow

hop

**18** What number should replace the question mark?

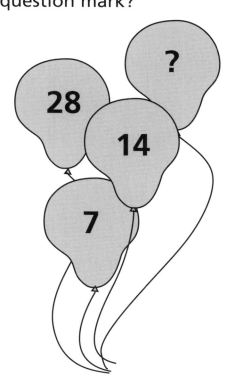

28

?

14

7

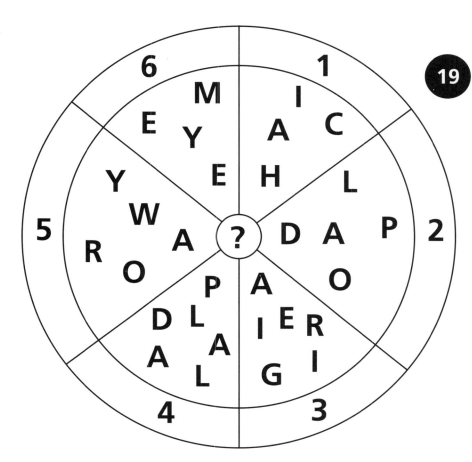

6

1

5

2

4

3

M
E
Y
I
C
A
H
E
L
Y
W
D
A
P
R
O
A
O
P
A
D
L
I
E
R
A
A
G
I
L

?

**19** The letters in each section of the circle form the name of a country if combined with the letter represented by the question mark.

**Can you name this letter, and also each of the countries?**

# LEVEL 4

**20** Insert the same even number into this sum three times so that the answer is correct.

$$3 + 1 \div 5 - 1 = 1$$

**21** Can you rearrange these boxes to form three nine-letter words?

| ASI | ARK | RAT |
|-----|-----|-----|
| WAT | IVE | ERM |
| NAR | TES | PAR |

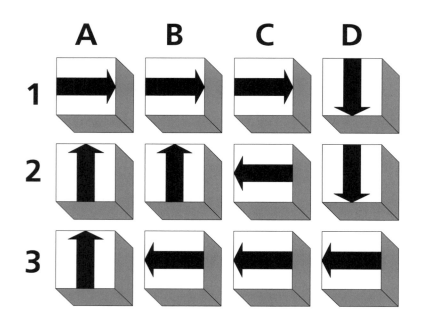

**22** On which square must you start in order to cover every square?

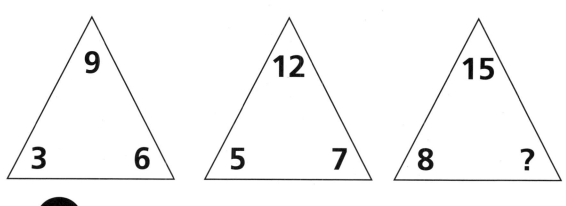

**23** What number should fill the blank space?

**24** Which number replaces the question mark?

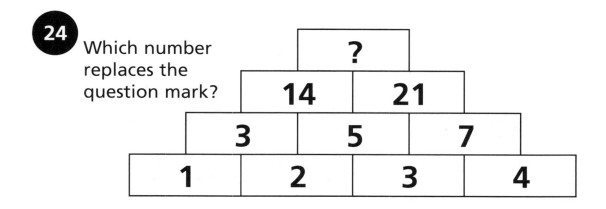

| 1 | 2 | 3 | 4 | 5 | 6 | 7 | 8 | 9 |
|---|---|---|---|---|---|---|---|---|
| A | B | C | D | E | F | G | H | I |
| J | K | L | M | N | O | P | Q | R |
| S | T | U | V | W | X | Y | Z |   |

**25** Can you use the table to find the name of a famous Formula 1 racing driver?

| 1 | 3 | 1 | 9 | 5 |
|---|---|---|---|---|
|   |   |   |   |   |

| 7 | 9 | 6 | 1 | 2 |
|---|---|---|---|---|
|   |   |   |   |   |

**1** This is a very sad story, though the evening started off in a quite ordinary way. Jessica had persuaded Philip to take her to the cinema to see a rather esoteric movie in which he had no interest at all. But being a rather good-natured chap, and because it was Jessica's birthday the next day, he agreed.

The film was certainly tedious – so much so that Philip dropped off after only 15 minutes. However, the dream he had while slumped in the cinema seat was far more exciting. He had returned to the time of the Crusades and was, as an infidel, being attacked by an invading army.

Suddenly, he found himself face-to-face with a swordsman who promptly cut off his head. Indeed, the dream was so realistic that Philip had a heart attack right there and then and died, without regaining consciousness. Jessica never got over his death.

**Do you believe this story, and if not, why not?**

**2** Can you find the odd one out?

| A | B | C | D | E |
|---|---|---|---|---|
| 1236 | 2147 | 5038 | 1023 | 4519 |

**3** One summer's evening, three rednecks met up at the village bench with the intention of sampling some beer.

Tom had a flagon containing five pints of beer; Jack had a jug containing three pints of beer; and Joe brought only an empty gallon jug, but promised to pay for all that the three of them drank.

The first two poured their beer into Joe's jug from which it was then shared out equally into identical glasses.

At last, when the final drop had been supped, and the three old-timers had finished putting the world to rights, they bid each other goodnight, and Joe placed eight dollar bills on the bench, telling his companions to sort out the finances for themselves.

As he walked away, however, Joe could hear Tom and Jack disagreeing over how the money should be allocated. He grinned to himself mischievously, as if this had been his plan all along. It would make a good talking point at their next get-together.

**How much, in fact, should each of Joe's friends have received, given that each had drunk no more than the other two men?**

**4** Which shape should be placed in the blank space – **A**, **B**, **C** or **D**?

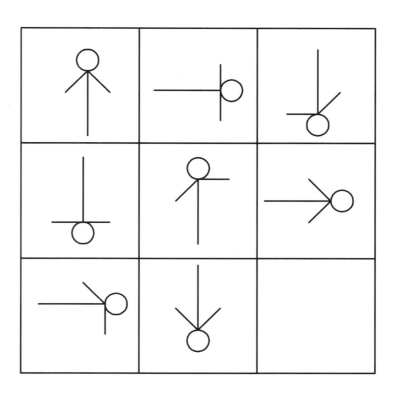

**5** Which of the following is not a bird?

1. WOLASLW
2. BNIOR
3. IGLNTAHGINE
4. OCSIHTR
5. RFAEFIG

**6** Can you use the table below to find the name of a famous building?

| 1 | 2 | 3 | 4 | 5 | 6 | 7 | 8 | 9 |
|---|---|---|---|---|---|---|---|---|
| A | B | C | D | E | F | G | H | I |
| J | K | L | M | N | O | P | Q | R |
| S | T | U | V | W | X | Y | Z | |

| 7 | 1 | 9 | 2 | 8 | 5 | 5 | 6 | 5 |
|---|---|---|---|---|---|---|---|---|

| | | | | | | | | |
|---|---|---|---|---|---|---|---|---|
| | | | | | | | | |

**7** Can you unscramble the letters to reveal two professions?

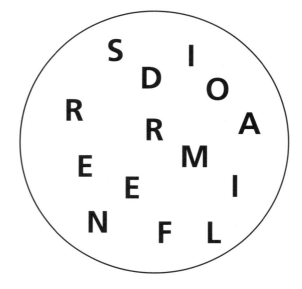

**8** If John's grandmother's age is a perfect square (for example, 49, which is 7 x 7), and her age equals the square of his father's age less the square of his mother's age, 40, what is the age of his grandmother?

**9** Can you work out which car belongs to which man? Note that some of the cars use leadfree petrol and others do not. Those that do not give out more exhaust.

James does not use leadfree petrol but his car has a radio. His hub caps are the same as Frank's.

Andrew's car has a radio, too, and his car has the same colour hub caps as Charlie's.

Charlie's car uses the same type of petrol as Edward's.

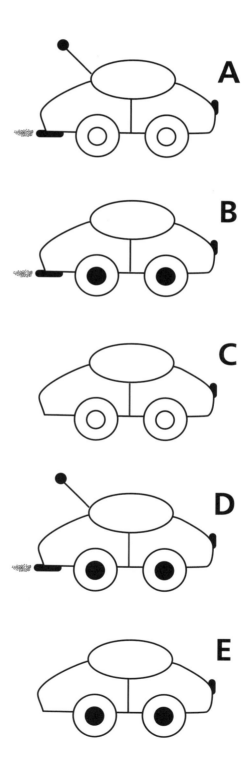

A

B

C

D

E

49

**10** Once, to test the intelligence of his knights, King Arthur set a task. He held out this shield and asked them to count how many complete squares the pattern thereon contained. Only the wisest of the novices counted correctly.

Can *you* calculate the number accurately?

**11** Back in his foolhardy days when George used to smoke – before, that is, he became aware of how it was affecting his health and when he was an impoverished student – he would always save his cigarette ends and then use them to roll some more.

Once he saved as many as 150 ends over a period. How many new cigarettes could he roll from these if he always needed 3 butts for 1 new cigarette?

| B | D | F | H | A | C | E | G | I |
|---|---|---|---|---|---|---|---|---|
| C | E | G | I | B | D | F | H | A |
| D | F | H | A | C | E | G | I | B |
| E | G | I |   |   |   | H | A | C |
| F | H | A |   |   |   | I | B | D |
| G | I | B |   |   |   | A | C | E |
| H | A | C | E | G | I | B | D | F |
| I | B | D | F | H | A | C | E | G |
| A | C | E | G | I | B | D | F | H |

**12** When the grid is complete, no letter will appear more than once in any horizontal row or vertical column. Which group of letters therefore completes the grid – **1**, **2**, **3** or **4**?

**1**

| D | F | H |
|---|---|---|
| E | G | I |
| F | H | A |

**2**

| B | D | F |
|---|---|---|
| C | E | G |
| D | F | H |

**3**

| B | F | D |
|---|---|---|
| C | E | G |
| D | H | F |

**4**

| B | D | F |
|---|---|---|
| C | H | G |
| D | F | E |

51

**13** Which shape fits the hole – **A**, **B**, **C** or **D**?
Shapes may be rotated but not flipped over.

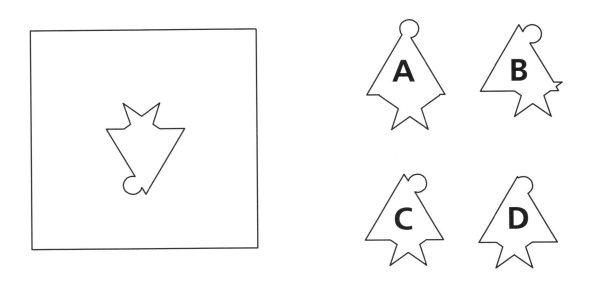

**14** What number should replace the
question mark in the floating boxes?

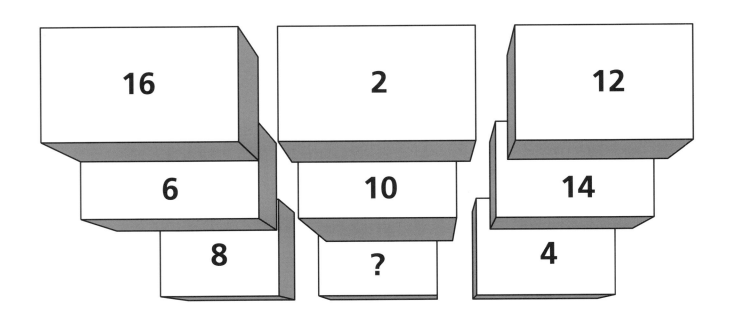

| B | D | C |
|---|---|---|
| H | A | F |
| G | E | I |

**15** Which letter lies one letter above the letter which is between the letters between B and G and C and I?

**16** Can you rearrange these boxes to form three nine-letter words?

| ACL | MAH | AVA |
|-----|-----|-----|
| BAR | IAN | JAH |
| ARA | BAR | BAL |

**17** What regular shape can be formed by rearranging the pieces shown?

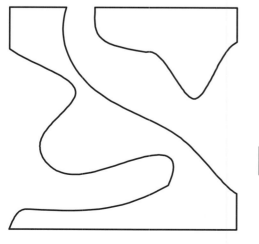
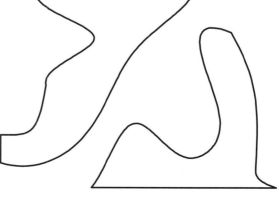

**18** Can you set out 24 matches so that you have 6 squares and 20 triangles in the arrangement?

**19** What number should replace the question mark?

| 2 | 1 | 4 | 7 |
|---|---|---|---|
| 3 | 4 | 2 | 9 |
| 4 | 1 | 1 | 6 |
| 2 | 0 | 6 | ? |

**20** Celia was something of a spendthrift, forever going down the shopping mall on a Saturday afternoon. One day, while on vacation in England, her husband was perturbed to find she had spent one-third of the money in their joint account, plus £200, in a single afternoon! They then had left only half what was originally in the account, plus £100.

**How much were they in credit before Celia spent so freely?**

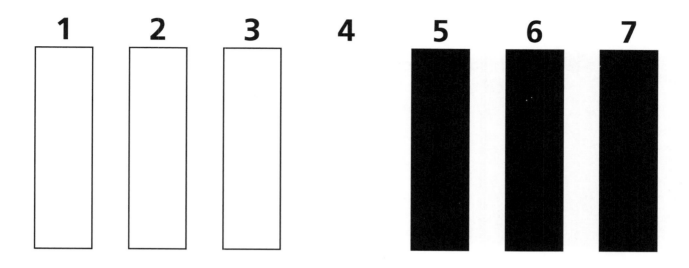

**1** The above layout shows three white blocks and three black blocks. Can you, by moving one block at a time to an adjacent position or by jumping over an adjacent block or space, completely change the position of the white blocks to that of the black blocks, and vice versa? Start by moving a white block.

**2** Three consecutive numbers when multiplied together give the answer 21,924.

**Can you work out which they are?**

| EST | ACH | TRE |
|-----|-----|-----|
| TIC | CEL | THE |
| IAL | ERY | AES |

**3** Can you find three 9-letter words by rearranging these boxes?

**4** Which shape should replace the question mark – **A**, **B**, **C** or **D**?

**5** What number completes the grid?

| 1 | 2 | 3 | 4 |
|---|---|---|---|
| 4 | 3 | 2 | 1 |
| 4 | 3 | 2 | 1 |
| 9 | ? | 7 | 6 |

**A**

**B**

**C**

**D**

**6** One of the bottom numbers is linked to one of the top letters. By starting with the numbered boxes, can you work out which two are linked? Every second arrow you land on is showing the exact *opposite* of the way you should go.

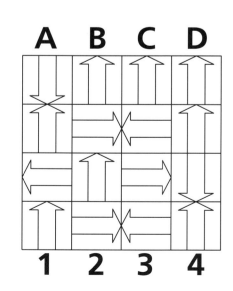

**7** One day, Mr Quiz laid six numbered counters on a table, as shown here. He then asked his wife if she could arrange them into two lines of three, by moving only two counters. His wife succeeded.

Mr Quiz next put the counters back in their original order, as shown, and asked if she could now arrange them in two rows of four, by moving only one counter. This time, his wife took somewhat longer. **Can you see the solutions to these two puzzles?**

**8** Which shape fits the hole – **A**, **B** or **C**?

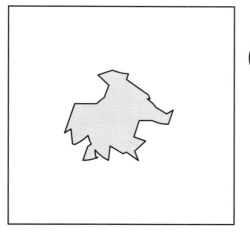

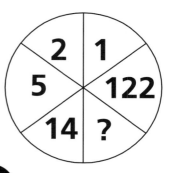

**9** What number should replace the question mark?

**10** What number should fill the blank space?

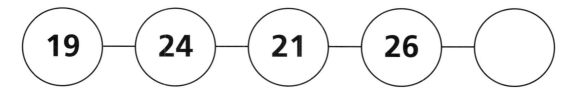

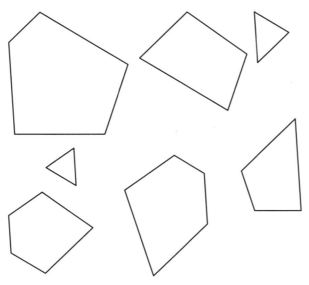

**11** What regular shape can be formed by rearranging the pieces shown left?

**12** Some time after asking his knights to work out how many complete squares there were in the pattern on the shield shown *right*, King Arthur asked his men how many rectangles could be found therein. Although this task was more difficult than the last, all of the knights managed to work it out, so King Arthur was most pleased. Can you do it, too?

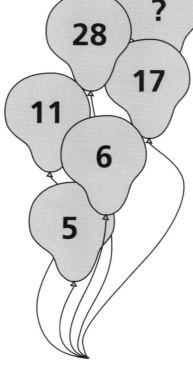

**13** What number should replace the question mark?

**14** Which shape comes next in the sequence – **A**, **B**, or **C**?

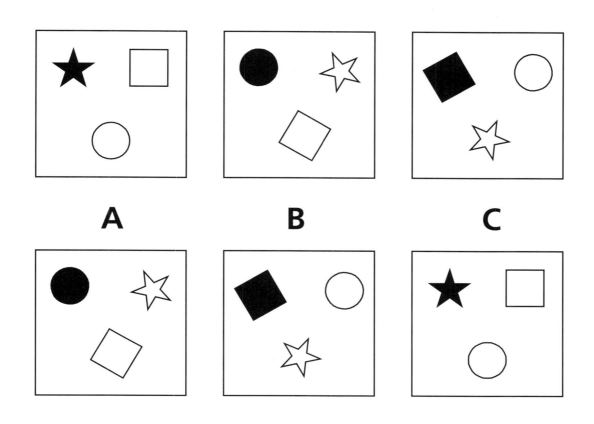

**A**      **B**      **C**

**15** Can you solve this puzzle? Choose from **A**, **B**, **C**, or **D**.

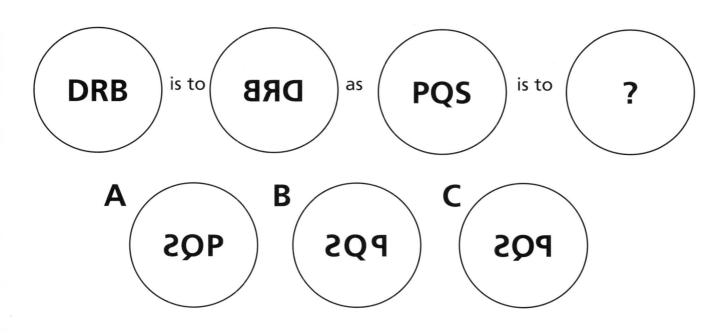

**16** A wealthy but eccentric widow left her three sons her 18 pedigree Siamese cats, each extremely valuable in its own right. Sadly, though, on the very day of the reading of the will, one of these beautiful beasts, past its prime, also passed away. This was all the more unfortunate because the widow had stipulated in her will that her favourite son should receive half of the cats, and the other two sons, one-third and one-ninth of the 18 cats respectively.

Can you suggest how they finally managed to get around the problem of dividing up the cats according to their mother's wishes, without resorting to slaughter or to shared ownership?

| A | P | F | Q | D |
|---|---|---|---|---|
| O | R | W | S | J |
| H | V | E | X | I |
| N | U | Y | T | K |
| B | M | G | L | C |

**17**
1. Which letter is two letters below **F**?
2. Which letter is to the left of the letter two places above **T**?
3. Which letter is above the letter three places to the left of the letter which is two places below the letter to the right of **X**?
4. Which letter lies in the middle of the letters which are between **F** and **I**, and **H** and **G**?

**18** Can you use the table to find the name of a famous British politician?

| 1 | 2 | 3 | 4 | 5 | 6 | 7 | 8 | 9 |
|---|---|---|---|---|---|---|---|---|
| A | B | C | D | E | F | G | H | I |
| J | K | L | M | N | O | P | Q | R |
| S | T | U | V | W | X | Y | Z |   |

| 5 | 9 | 5 | 1 | 2 | 6 | 5 |
|---|---|---|---|---|---|---|
|   |   |   |   |   |   |   |

| 3 | 8 | 3 | 9 | 3 | 8 | 9 | 3 | 3 |
|---|---|---|---|---|---|---|---|---|
|   |   |   |   |   |   |   |   |   |

**19** Which dial comes next in the series **A**, **B**, **C**, or **D**?

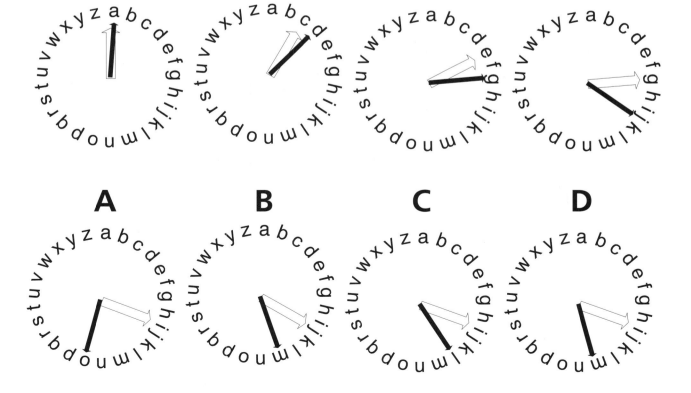

**A**     **B**     **C**     **D**

**20** What number should replace the question mark?

**21** What number should be placed centrally in the last triangle?

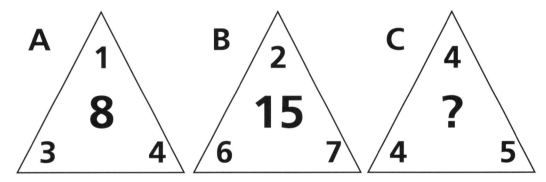

**22** What is the sum total of the spots on the hidden vertical faces of these three dice?

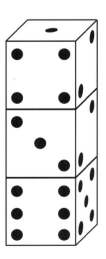

**23** What number replaces the question mark?

| 27 | 2 | 1 | 125 | 6 |
|----|---|---|-----|---|
| 3 | 8 | 1 | 5 | ? |

**24** Take 10 playing cards and arrange them as shown, face-down. The aim is to touch one card, jump over the two cards that are adjacent to it in a clockwise direction, and then turn over the next card. Keep on doing this, moving over the two adjacent cards whether or not they have been turned over and always in a clockwise direction, until only one card is left face-down. Can you do it? You will need to discover the correct sequence of moves that will make it possible to be left with one card not turned up.

**25** Sylvia Johnson popped into the supermarket and bought just two items – a birthday cake for her son, Jeremy, and a packet of biscuits. At the check-out, she paid with a $10 note and a 50 cent piece and got no change.

Looking at the till receipt, she noticed that the cake had cost six times as much as the biscuits.

**How much had they cost respectively?**

**26** What number should replace the question mark?

|  | 36 |  |   |  | 84 |  |   |  | 96 |  |
|---|----|---|---|---|----|---|---|----|----|---|
| 3 | 18 | 6 |   | 7 | 21 | 3 | 12 | ? | 4 |
|  | 2 |  |   |  | 4 |  |   |  | 2 |  |

**27** Can you identify the odd one out?

A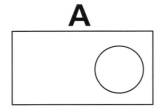

B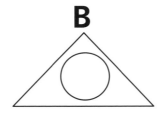

C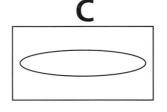

D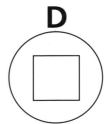

E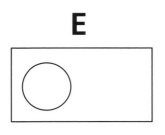

F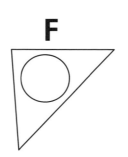

G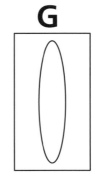

H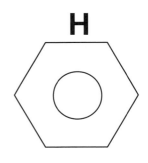

**1** Can you assign numerical values (all whole numbers lower than 10) to the shapes □, ○ and △ so that the see-saws are perfectly balanced. You should then once more be able to work out what replaces the question mark – **A**, **B** or **C**.

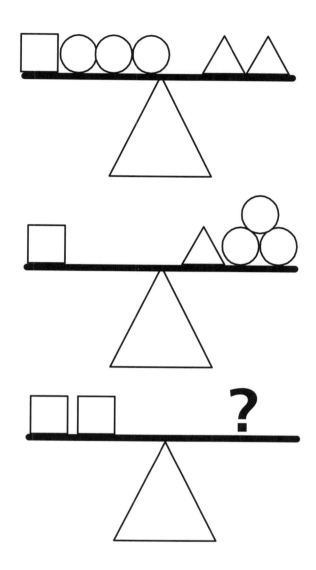

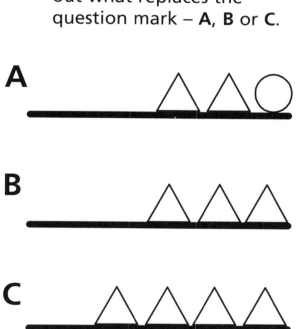

**A**

**B**

**C**

**2** Which letter is to the left of the letter which is two places below the letter two places to the right of E?

| A | B | C | D |
| E | F | G | H |
| I | J | K | L |
| M | N | O | P |

**3** In 14 years' time, William will be half the age of his father now and 9 years younger than his mother is now.

If his father is currently 34, how old is William now and how old is his mother?

65

**4** What number should replace the question mark?

**5** Sir Henry Duckdown was a little-known war correspondent in the early part of the 19th century, who once found himself standing on a battlefield, peering through his tripod-mounted telescope, as the opposing forces gathered before the conflict began. Carefully, he noted down the number of men and weapons on each side.

The army on his left comprised 2,000 infantry, 330 cavalry, 107 splendid cannons, each manned by three artillery men, and 50 mortars, each manned by two artillery men.

The army on his right, meanwhile, comprised 1,500 infantry, 400 cavalry, 75 cannons and 60 mortars The cannons and mortars were manned exactly as the army on his left. Then, suddenly, as a crack of cannon fire was heard, it was time for Sir Henry to make a speedy retreat.

**Can you calculate how many legs were on the battlefield when that first shot was fired?**

**6** Which shape fits the hole – **A**, **B**, **C** or **D**?

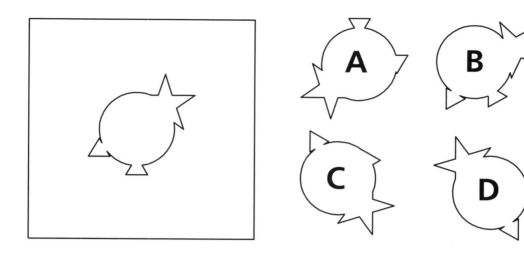

**7** There is always hot competition among anglers who are forever boasting about the size of the fish they have caught.

Norman was no exception; so when he announced that he had caught a whopper the previous day, everyone took it with a pinch of salt.

Its head, he said, was 5cm (2in) long. But that was not all. The tail was the length of its head plus half the body length; and the body was as long as the head and the tail together.

If we are generous and give Norman the benefit of the doubt, what was the total length of the fish he was describing?

**8**

Four young boys have been accused of daubing graffiti on the school wall. The headmaster calls them into his study and sets about trying to find the culprit by asking them each a question, knowing full well that only *one* of them would be telling the truth.

**Billy** says that **Rupert** did it.

**Rupert** says that **Douglas** did it.

**Douglas** says that **Rupert** is lying.

**Michael** is adamant and says that he didn't do it.

**Can you tell from their statements who actually drew the graffiti?**

**9** Can you find the odd letter out?

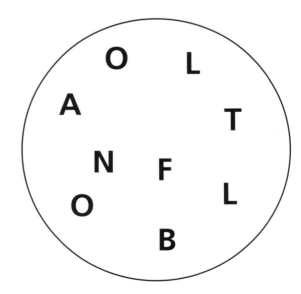

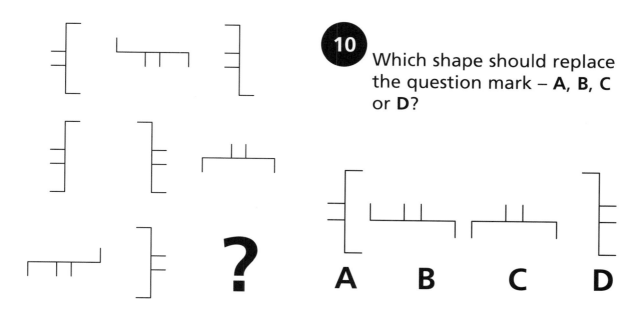

**10** Which shape should replace the question mark – **A**, **B**, **C** or **D**?

A    B    C    D

**11** Arrange the numbers 1-16 inclusive, one per square, to complete the equations. Each equation is solved in the order in which the numbers appear, eg the equation 13 + 5 ÷ 2 x 6 = 54 would be solved as 13 + 5 (=18) ÷ 2 (=9) x 6 = 54. Four numbers have been placed to start you off.

| 2 | − |    | + |    | + |    | = | 28 |
|---|---|----|---|----|---|----|---|----|
| x |   | +  |   | +  |   | −  |   |    |
|   | x | 11 | + |    | ÷ |    | = | 13 |
| − |   | +  |   | −  |   | +  |   |    |
|   | + |    | − | 13 | + |    | = | 4  |
| + |   | −  |   | x  |   | −  |   |    |
|   | + |    | − |    | ÷ | 3  | = | 8  |
| = |   | =  |   | =  |   | =  |   |    |
| 28|   | 3  |   | 36 |   | 7  |   |    |

**12** Which of the following is not a vegetable?

## 1. TRAORC
## 2. RNPPSAI
## 3. EDWSE
## 4. AOMTTO
## 5. LYCREE

**13** Which one comes next in the series this time – **A**, **B**, **C** or **D**?

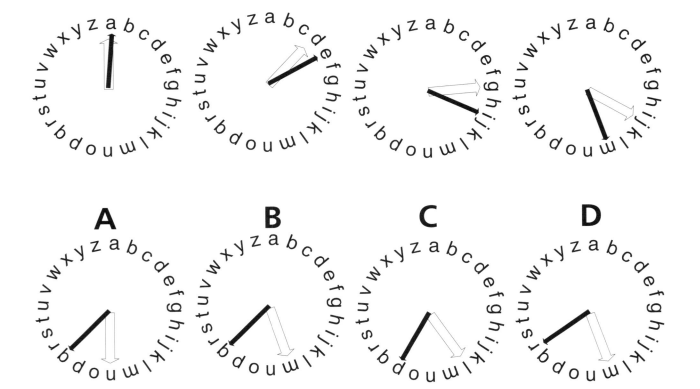

**A**          **B**          **C**          **D**

**14** What regular shape can be formed by rearranging the pieces shown?

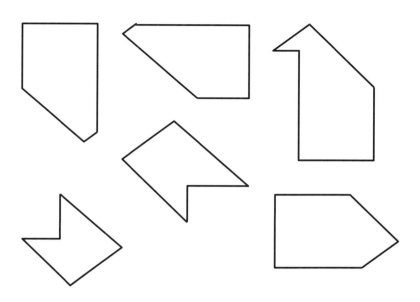

| CIG | GUE | TTE |
|-----|-----|-----|
| LEA | SCA | GER |
| ARE | VEN | COL |

**15** Can you rearrange these boxes to form three nine-letter words?

**16** What number should replace the question mark?

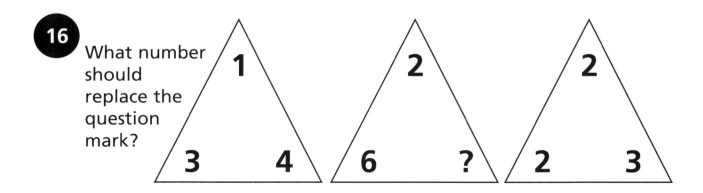

**17** Deborah went to the January sales with $100 cash in her purse, hoping she would find some bargains.

Her luck was in: she found some lovely silk scarves, marked down to $5 each, which would be ideal for friends and family for next Christmas; tights reduced to $1 per pair; and some beautiful beads, at just 5 cents each, so that she could make an exquisite necklace very cheaply.

Can you tell how many of each item she bought if she purchased 100 items altogether and spent all her money?

**18** Can you unscramble the letters to reveal two types of food?

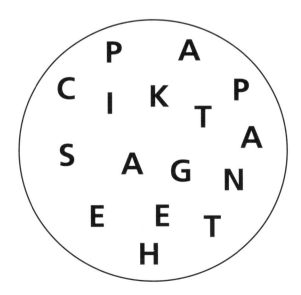

| 1 | 2 | 3 | 4 | 5 | 6 | 7 |
|---|---|---|---|---|---|---|
| A | B | C | D | E | F | G |
| H | I | J | K | L | M | N |
| O | P | Q | R | S | T | U |
| V | W | X | Y | Z |   |   |

**19** Can you use the table to find the name of a famous ship?

| 4 | 1 | 2 | 7 | 2 | 1 | 2 |
|---|---|---|---|---|---|---|
|   |   |   |   |   |   |   |

| 2 | 1 | 4 | 4 | 2 | 1 | 4 |
|---|---|---|---|---|---|---|
|   |   |   |   |   |   |   |

**20** Jim is 36 years old.

Gavin's wife is 33, and 3 years older than Rosie, and Helen is one year Eleanor's senior.

Mervin is 30 next birthday and 5 years older than his wife, and Rosie is the same age as her husband.

Sarah is 33 and Spike's wife is Rosie.

Laura is 27 and her husband, Jim, is a plumber.

Mervin's wife is 24 and thus 8 years Gavin's junior.

Helen's husband is Grant and he is one year younger than Mervin.

**Can you pair up the couples and give everyone's age?**

**21** Can you tell how to get 10 dancers to line up in five straight rows so that there are four in each row?

**22** How many squares are in this grid?

**23** Don't let this one tie you up in knots, to coin a phrase, but how could you possibly tie a knot in a piece of string while holding it with two hands without letting go of either end?

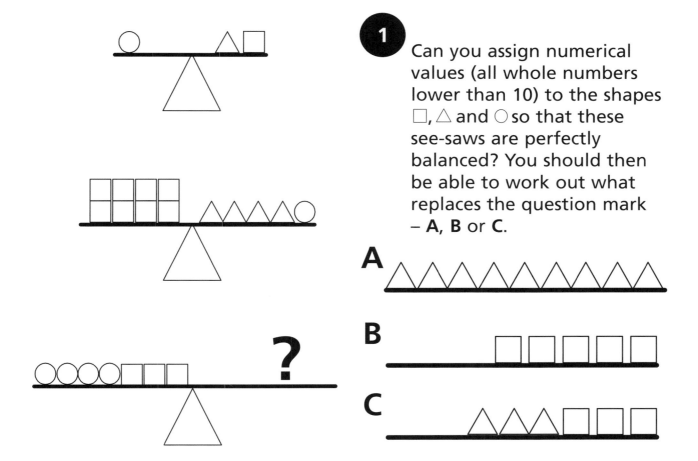

**1** Can you assign numerical values (all whole numbers lower than 10) to the shapes □, △ and ○ so that these see-saws are perfectly balanced? You should then be able to work out what replaces the question mark – **A**, **B** or **C**.

**A**

**B**

**C**

**2** Don and Doris keep hens and are very proud of them.

They are generous with the eggs that the hens lay and every week take some to the local old folks' home.

One afternoon, as they handed some to the matron, she asked how many hens they had.

"Well", replied Doris, ever one to make things more complicated than they need to be, "if we had twice the number, plus half the number, plus one hen more, we would have 26 in all."

The matron looked utterly confused.

Can you enlighten her?

**3** What number should replace the question mark?

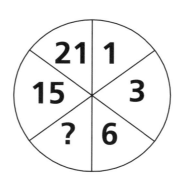

**4** In each horizontal row and vertical column, can you replace the question marks by a multiplication, division, addition or subtraction sign, so that the total at the end of each line is correct?

6 ? 7 ? 4 ? 3 = 41
?   ?   ?   ?
4 ? 3 ? 9 ? 8 = 55
?   ?   ?   ?
9 ? 5 ? 2 ? 1 = 46
?   ?   ?   ?
3 ? 6 ? 8 ? 5 = 50

=   =   =   =

11   20   10   5

**5**

In this puzzle, you need to work out the year in question. It has four digits.

The sum of the first and second digits equals the third.

The second digit less the fourth equals the first.

The first multiplied by the second equals the second.

Add the third to the fourth and you get twice the second.

Add the first and the fourth and you get the second.

Subtract the first from the second and you get the fourth.

Multiply the second by the third, add together the figures in the two-digit result, and you get the third.

Multiply the third by the fourth, add together the figures in the two-digit result, and you get the third.

**6**

Which letter completes the above statement?

# M is to N T is to

# W, K, I or Z

**7** Which is the odd man out?

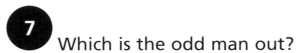

| A | B | C | D |
|---|---|---|---|
| COTTON | SILK | LINEN | HESSIAN |

**8** Which shape fits the hole – **A**, **B**, **C** or **D**?

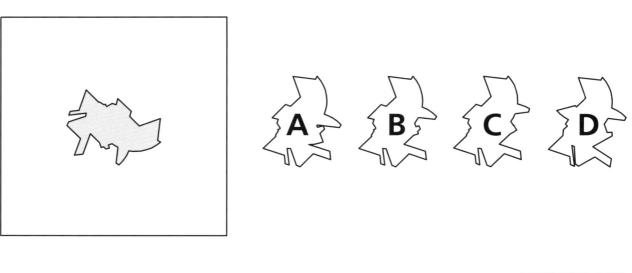

**9** Which number will complete the series that starts below?

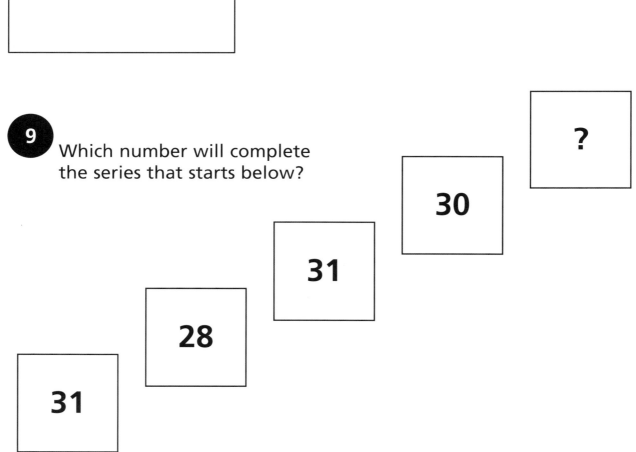

31

28

31

30

?

**10** What numbers should fill the final diamond shape?

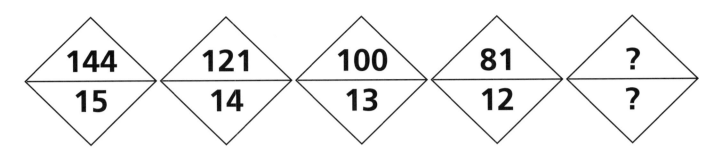

| 144 | 121 | 100 | 81 | ? |
| 15 | 14 | 13 | 12 | ? |

**11** Which letter is two places to the left of the letter which is one place below the letter which is between J and D?

| A | B | C | D |
| E | F | G | H |
| I | J | K | L |
| M | N | O | P |

**12** Can you unscramble the letters to reveal two animals?

**13** Tony always has a problem remembering the code on the lock to his smart new leather briefcase.

What he *can* recall, however, is that it comprises two 3s, separated by 3 other figures; two 2s, separated by 2 figures; and two 1s, separated by one figure only.

The problem is, however, that there are two possible combinations. Tony needs the higher number for his case.

Can you work out what it is?

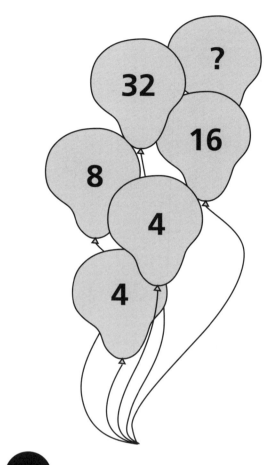

**14** What number should replace the question mark?

**15** Would you eat, wear, carry or talk to the following anagram?

# LARLEBUM

**16** Can you find the odd one out? Is it **A, B, C, D** or **E**?

| A | B | C | D | E |
|---|---|---|---|---|
| 1367 | 2343 | 1579 | 2378 | 5789 |

**17** Can you rearrange these boxes to form three nine-letter words?

| UPA | TED | NTS |
|-----|-----|-----|
| HAN | ILS | COC |
| KTA | OCC | ENC |

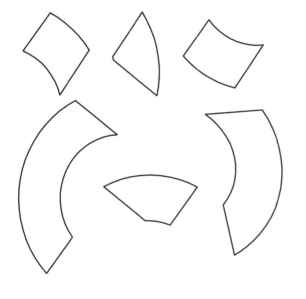

**18** Which letter do these pieces form when rearranged?

**19** What number should replace the question mark?

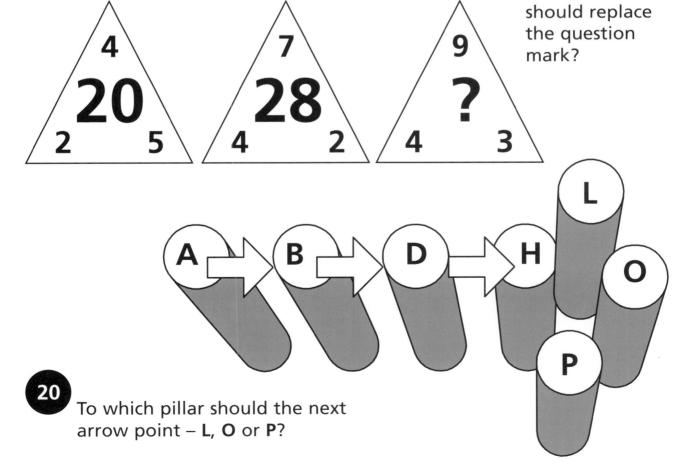

**20** To which pillar should the next arrow point – **L**, **O** or **P**?

**21** Take 8 coins. Place one on any numbered point of the figure shown here and slide it to the end of either of the two lines that run from it.

Leave it there. Then do the same thing with a second coin, and so on.

Carry on doing this and see if you can succeed in leaving just one point uncovered, with one coin left.

Can you discover the way to achieve this?

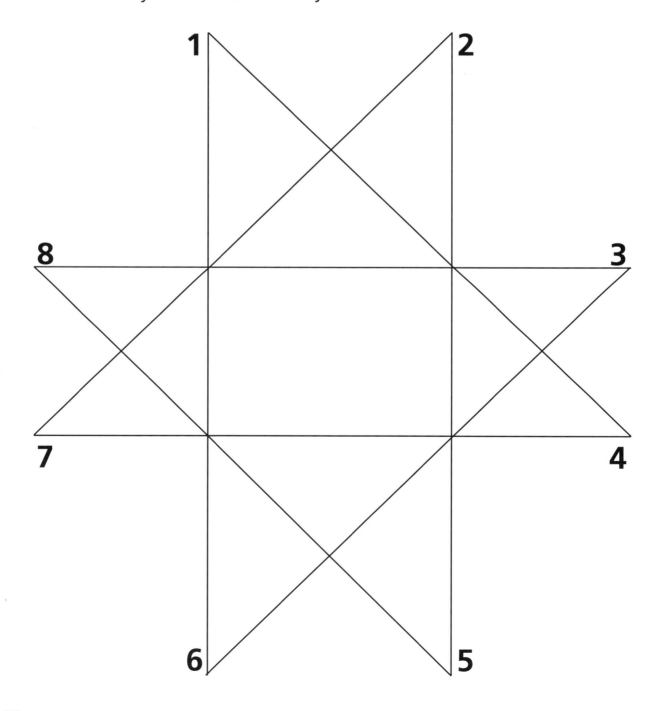

**22** Which letter should replace the question mark?

# L/E  P/F  V/A
# M/S  O/N  W/?

| 1 | 5 | 7 | 6 | 13 |
|---|---|---|---|---|
| 4 | 5 | 8 | 14 | ? |

**23** What numbers should replace the question mark?

**24** Which dial comes next in this series – **A**, **B**, **C** or **D**?

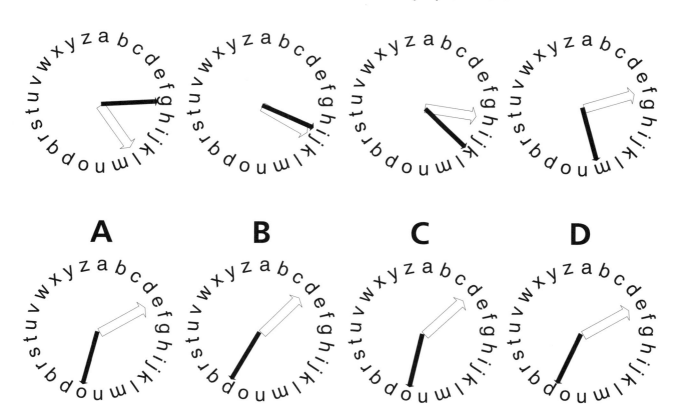

**A**　　　**B**　　　**C**　　　**D**

**1** What single-figure number should replace the question mark?

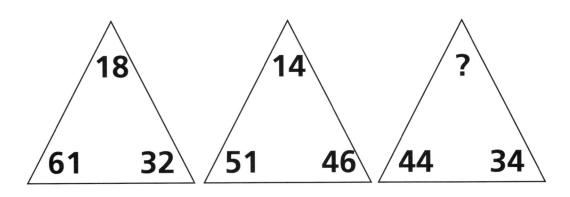

**2** Look at the subdivided square shown here.
Can you think how to put 12 spots in the small squares so that there are only 2 spots in every horizontal, vertical or diagonal line of two or more squares?

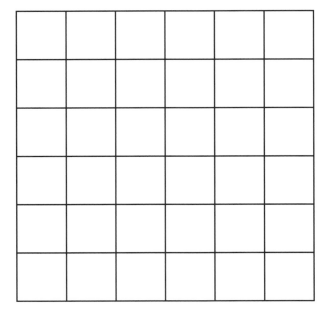

**3** Can you translate the following coded message?

# UGF ESNOS MHOD XHMK NNWD UNNNSQPV

**4** A woman goes into a café and orders a cup of hot chocolate. As she can see from the menu, it is $1 with cream and 90 cents without, and she opts for the cream.

While she is standing at the counter, a man comes in, also asks for a hot chocolate, puts down $1 and is automatically given cream even though he didn't ask for it and in spite of the fact that he had never been into the café before.

**How did the waitress know that he wanted cream?**

**5** What links the outer numbers to the inner one?

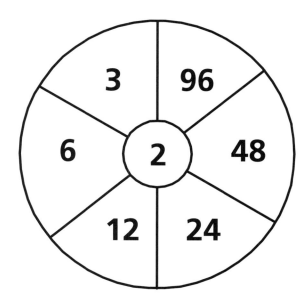

**6**

On the Planet Fantasia, different countries have different currencies, just as they do on Planet Earth.

The present rate of exchange is as follows:
6 zeds = 40 rambams;
50 rambams = 186 fobs;
54 fobs = 10 lentis;
124 lentis = 270 grobs.

**Can you calculate how many grobs there are to 1 zed?**

**7**

Use the table below to find the name of a mountain.

| 1 | 2 | 3 | 4 | 5 | 6 | 7 |
|---|---|---|---|---|---|---|
| A | B | C | D | E | F | G |
| H | I | J | K | L | M | N |
| O | P | Q | R | S | T | U |
| V | W | X | Y | Z |   |   |

| 4 | 2 | 5 | 2 | 6 | 1 | 7 | 3 | 1 | 4 | 1 |
|---|---|---|---|---|---|---|---|---|---|---|
|   |   |   |   |   |   |   |   |   |   |   |

**8** Which letter comes three places later in the alphabet than the letter that is (in a straight line) three places away from the letter which is two places above I, and two places away from the letter which is three places to the right of I?

| A | B | C | D |
|---|---|---|---|
| E | F | G | H |
| I | J | K | L |
| M | N | O | P |

**9** Can you unscramble the letters to reveal two types of transportation?

**10** Which dial comes next in this series – **A, B, C** or **D**?

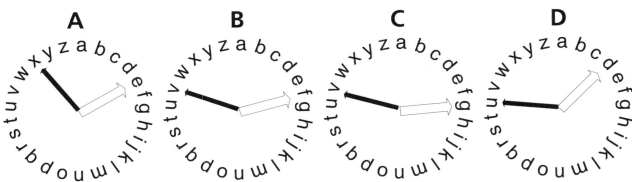

| A | B | C | D |

| TEB | HER | IST |
|-----|-----|-----|
| BOA | WHI | THO |
| BAL | USE | AIT |

**11** Can you rearrange this set of boxes to form three nine-letter words?

**12** What letter do these pieces form when rearranged?

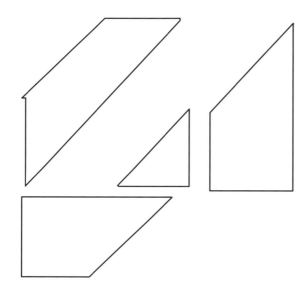

**13** If one number is taken from another, the answer is 4.

If one is squared and then subtracted from the square of the other, the answer is 48.

**Can you work out what the two numbers must be?**

**14** What number replaces the question mark?

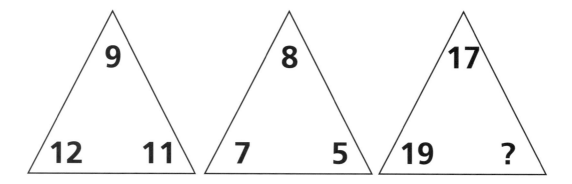

**15** This is a jewel of a question!
Can you find the odd man out?

| A | B | C | D | E |
|---|---|---|---|---|
| AMBER | DIAMOND | RUBY | EMERALD | TOPAZ |

**16** Can you use the logic of the first diagram to complete the one to the right of it?

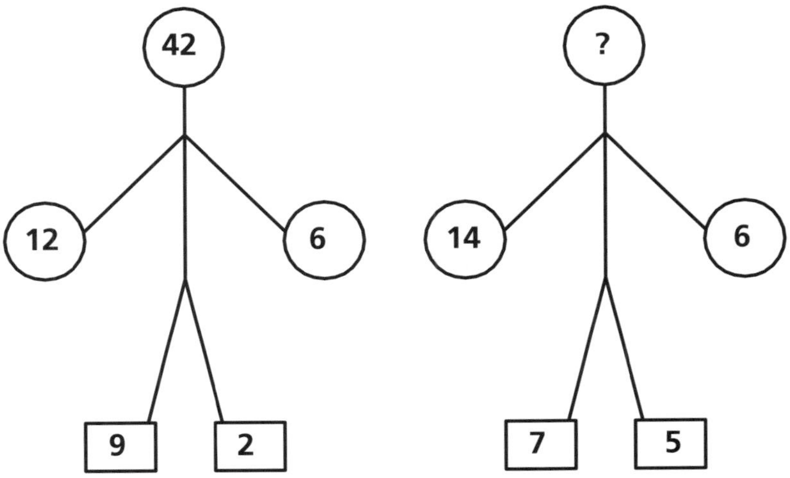

42
12   6
9   2

?
14   6
7   5

**17** It was a wonderful double wedding.

Ruth and her sister Jill were marrying Oliver and Gordon, who were both brothers. The odd thing, though, was that the girls would not have the same mother-in-law.

**Can you work out why?**

| | | | | | | |
|---|---|---|---|---|---|---|
| β | δ | φ | α | χ | ε | γ |
| χ | | γ | β | δ | φ | α |
| δ | | | χ | ε | γ | β |
| ε | γ | | | φ | α | χ |
| φ | α | χ | ε | γ | β | δ |
| γ | β | δ | φ | α | χ | ε |
| α | χ | ε | γ | β | δ | φ |

**18** Take a look at the above grid. Which group of tiles completes the grid – **A**, **B** or **C**?

**A**

| δ | |
|---|---|
| β | α |
| | φ | ε |

**B**

| | ε |
|---|---|
| φ | β |
| α | δ |

**C**

| ε | |
|---|---|
| φ | α |
| | β | δ |

**19** What number should be inserted in the empty box?

| 2 | 4 | 8 | 14 | 29 |
|---|---|----|----|----|
| 3 | 6 | 12 | 26 |    |

**20** Rupert was exhausted and decided to go straight to bed when he got home at 10.15pm, after visiting his mother.

He wound his bedside clock and set the alarm for 11 – luckily it was Saturday and he could sleep in on Sunday morning – and dropped off as soon as his head hit the pillow.

**How much sleep did he get before his slumbers were broken?**

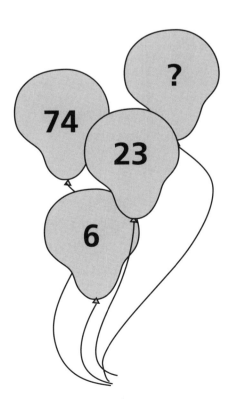

**21** What number should replace the question mark?

**22** Which shape fits the hole
– **A**, **B**, **C** or **D**?

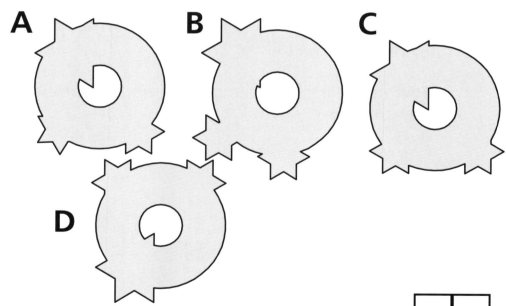

**23**

There are two books, volumes I and II of
a series, side by side on a shelf placed
vertically and with their spines facing us.
There is no space between the books.

Each of these has covers that are 10mm thick, and the total
thickness of the pages in each is 6mm. How far will a bookworm
travel if it starts from the first page in the first volume and travels
to the last page in the second volume?

**24** Once again, can you assign numerical values (all whole numbers lower than 20) to the shapes □, △ and ○ so that the see-saws are perfectly balanced? You should then be able to work out what replaces the question mark – **A**, **B** or **C**.

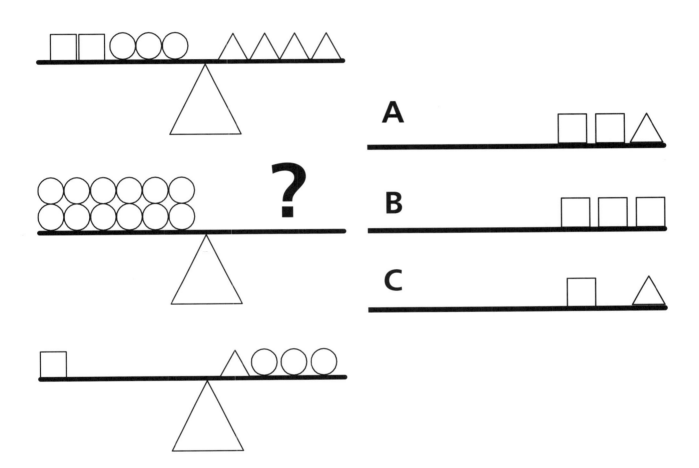

**25** Seven-year-old Paul has a box of 50 sweets and three friends – Amy, Sally and Eddie – among whom to share them. He is so generous that he decides only to take one sweet for himself each time he has doled out 10.

Paul starts to hand them out one at a time, starting with Amy, next Sally, and then Eddie; but every fourth sweet he hands out is also accompanied by an extra one for that particular friend.

**How many sweets does each finally receive?**

**1** Which letter do these pieces form when rearranged?

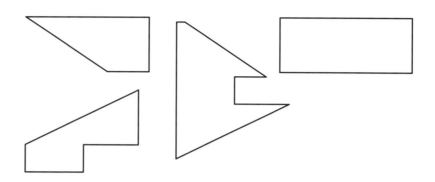

| HAR | FTS | LET |
|-----|-----|-----|
| ERS | CON | CRA |
| FAL | MEN | GIC |

**2** Can you rearrange these boxes to form three nine-letter words?

**3** What number should replace the question mark?

| 6 | 7 | 9 | 10 | 12 |
|----|----|----|----|----|
| 15 | 25 | 36 | 46 | ? |

**4** Which dial comes next in the series – **A, B, C** or **D**?

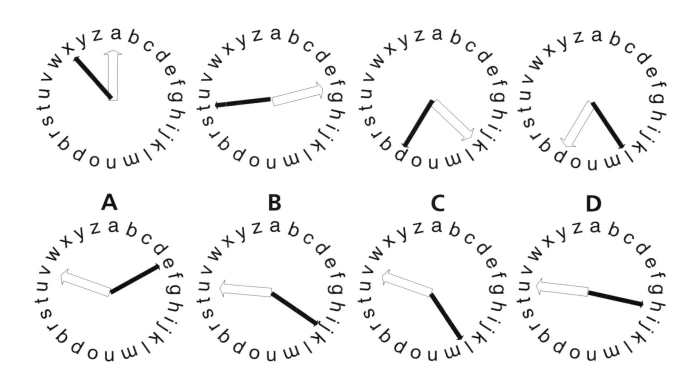

**A**    **B**    **C**    **D**

**5** Can you determine which of the following jumbled words is the odd one out?

# 1. RUAHRBB    4. OLECAOHTC

# 2. ANBNAA    5. NLEPAIPPE

# 3. CTRNNIAEE    6. RITPGUEFAR

**6** If Beethoven scores 3,
Delius scores 1,
Brahms scores 0
and Weber scores 2,
what is Elgar's score?

**7** What links
the outer
numbers to
the inner
one?

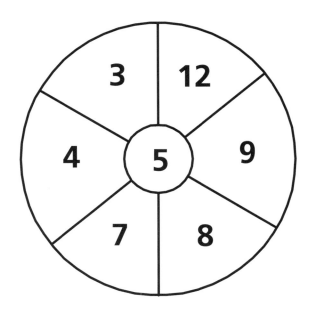

**8**
A tourist walking through the streets of a run-down quarter of Paris was beset at every corner by beggars.

At the first corner, he gave a poor man and his dog one euro more than half the money that he had in his trouser pocket. After all, the chap looked half-starved, and so did his pet.

Five minutes later, a tramp approached him, and the tourist gave this bedraggled figure 2 euros more than half of what he had left.

Then 3 minutes later, he gave away 3 euros more than half of what was left to an old woman.

Now, when he felt in his pocket, he found he had only one euro left for himself!

**Can you calculate how much money the tourist had in his pocket to start with?**

**9** Which box replaces the question mark – **A**, **B** or **C**?

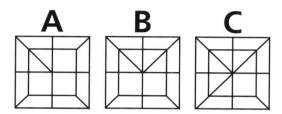

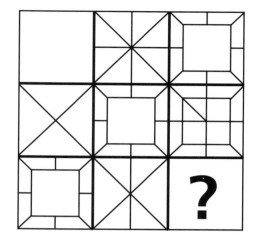

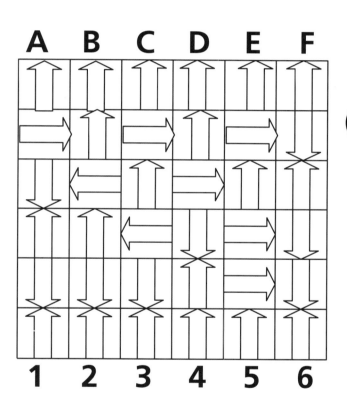

**10** One of the bottom numbers is linked to one of the top letters. By starting with the numbered boxes, can you work out which two are linked? By the way, every second arrow you land on is showing the exact *opposite* of the way you *should* go.

**11** What number replaces the question mark?

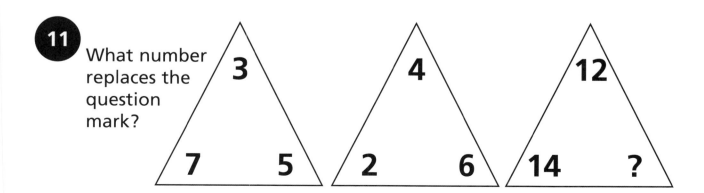

**12** Four friends – a doctor, a lawyer, a professor and a dentist – decided to try a new restaurant for lunch. After a pleasant meal, the waiter, who was in the kitchen, could hear the four discussing whose turn it was to pay. Eventually, the lawyer decided to settle up with a credit card and shouted for the bill. The waiter promptly came from the kitchen and placed the bill in front of the lawyer.

If the waiter had never seen any of the friends before, how did he know he was giving the bill to the correct person?

**13** Can you rearrange the blocks to form a magic square? Each horizontal, vertical and diagonal row should add up to 95.

| 10 |    |    |
|----|----|----|
| 12 | 11 | 30 |
|    |    | 7  |

|    | 25 |    |
|----|----|----|
| 8  | 27 |    |
| 15 | 9  |    |

|    |    | 16 |
|----|----|----|
| 24 | 18 |    |
| 31 |    |    |

| 29 | 23 |

|    |    | 14 |
|----|----|----|
| 28 | 22 | 21 |

| 19 | 13 |
|----|----|
| 26 | 20 |

| 17 |

**14** If apples cost 69 cents per kilo, oranges cost 79 cents per kilo and bananas cost 52 cents per kilo, how much does 1/2 kilo of grapes cost? Yes, there is some logic to this question!

| 1 | 2 | 3 | 4 | 5 | 6 |
|---|---|---|---|---|---|
| A | B | C | D | E | F |
| G | H | I | J | K | L |
| M | N | O | P | Q | R |
| S | T | U | V | W | X |
| Y | Z |   |   |   |   |

**15** Use the table below to find the title of a play by Shakespeare.

| 2 | 2 | 5 |
|---|---|---|
|   |   |   |

| 1 | 5 | 6 | 3 | 2 | 1 | 2 | 2 |
|---|---|---|---|---|---|---|---|
|   |   |   |   |   |   |   |   |

| 3 | 6 |
|---|---|
|   |   |

| 4 | 5 | 2 | 3 | 3 | 5 |
|---|---|---|---|---|---|
|   |   |   |   |   |   |

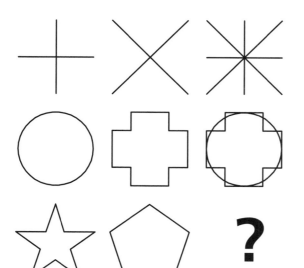

**?**

**16** Which shape replaces the question mark – **A**, **B**, **C** or **D**?

**A**      **B**      **C**

  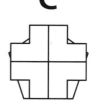

**17** Which box differs in one respect from all the rest?

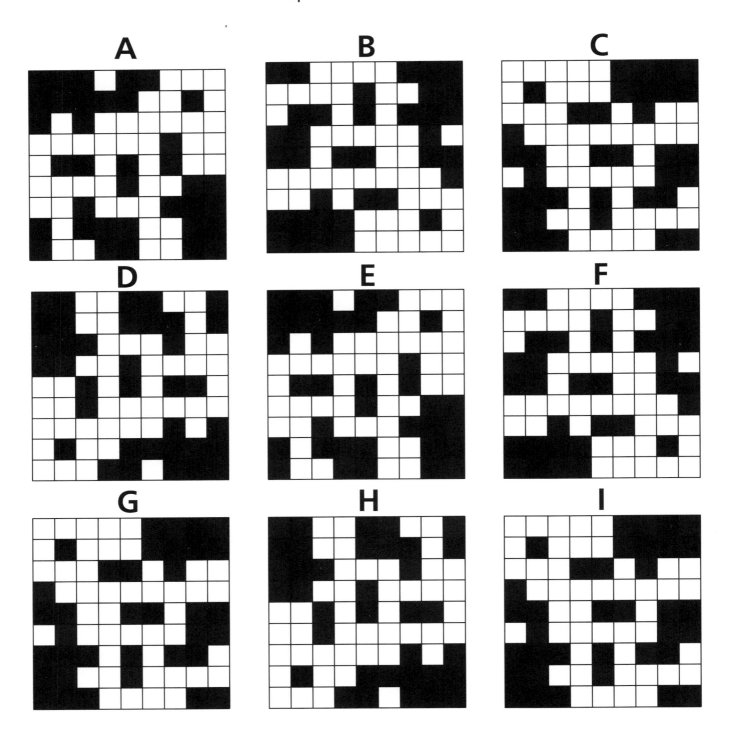

A  B  C

D  E  F

G  H  I

**1** Geraldine has a most magnificent garden, with a colourful border along the whole of one side. In this border, there is a splendid display – 4,070 plants in total, all neatly laid out in rows. No wonder she has won so many competitions! In a very precise way, Geraldine has planted 160 pansies in the first row, and 580 delphiniums in the last row, and various different rows of plants in between. The number of plants in each row behind the first row exceeds those in the row in front of it by a definite number each time. From the above information, can you work out how many rows there are altogether in the prize border?

**2** **5631829271** is to **4823748463** as **3295871652** is to one of the following – **A**, **B**, **C** or **D**. Which is it?

**A. 2384762763**
**B. 2487790844**
**C. 2186962741**
**D. 4306760543**

**3** What is one-half of two-thirds of three-quarters of four-fifths of five-sixths of six-sevenths of seven-eighths of eight-ninths of nine-tenths of 10,000?

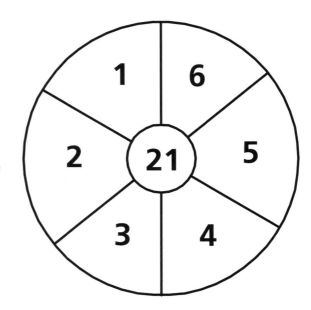

**4** What links the
outside number
to the inner one?

**5** What number replaces the
question mark?

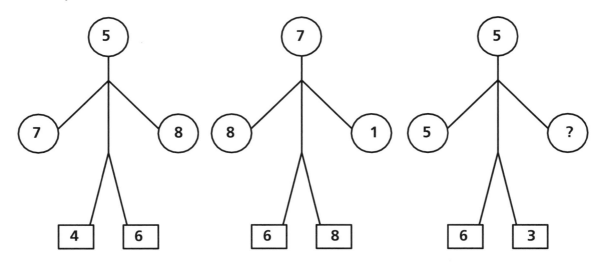

**6** Which shape fits the hole – **A**, **B**, **C** or **D**?

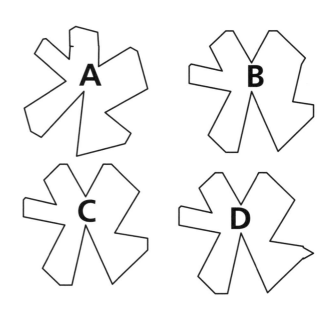

**7** What number completes the diagram?

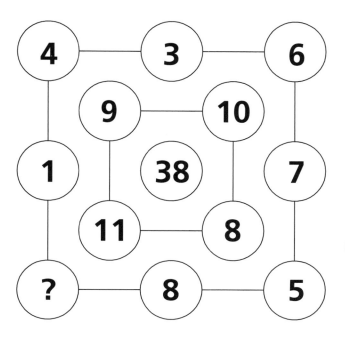

**8** What number should replace the question mark?

**9** Use the table to find the name of a famous artist.

| 1 | 2 | 3 | 4 | 5 | 6 |
|---|---|---|---|---|---|
| A | B | C | D | E | F |
| G | H | I | J | K | L |
| M | N | O | P | Q | R |
| S | T | U | V | W | X |
| Y | Z |   |   |   |   |

| 1 | 3 | 3 | 2 | 5 | 6 | 1 | 2 | 1 | 5 | 6 | 3 |
|---|---|---|---|---|---|---|---|---|---|---|---|
|   |   |   |   |   |   |   |   |   |   |   |   |

**10** Which letter do these pieces form when rearranged?

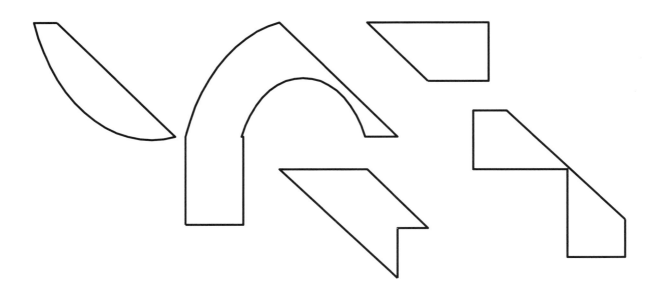

| 2 | 5 | 7 | 8 |
|---|---|---|---|
| 3 | 6 | 7 | 3 |
| 4 | 4 | 7 | 2 |
| 1 | 7 | 7 | ? |

**11** What number completes the grid?

**12** Can you rearrange these boxes to form three nine-letter words?

| STR | NTW | IAT |
|-----|-----|-----|
| PAN | TYM | ORK |
| ION | IST | PAI |

**13** Which box differs in one respect from all the rest?

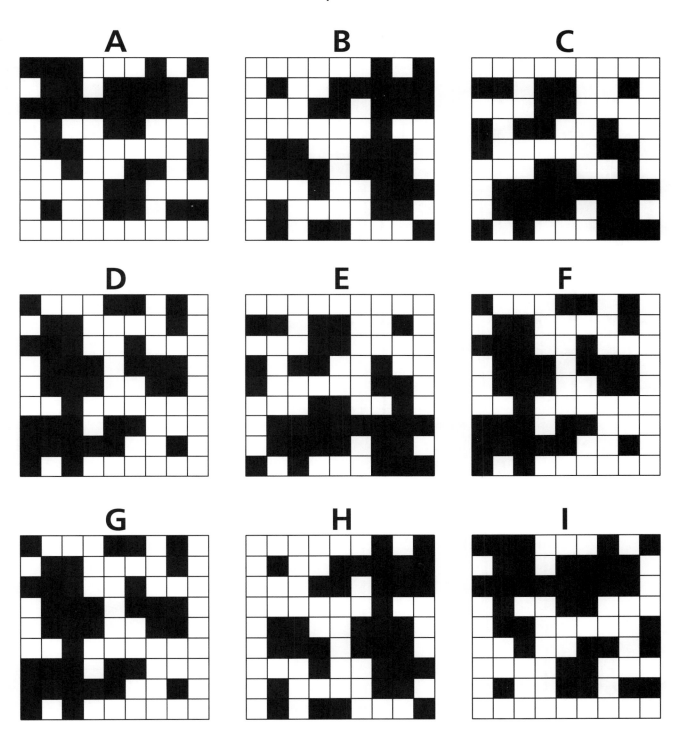

A  B  C

D  E  F

G  H  I

**14** If two bags of sand and three bags of sugar weigh 10kg (22lb), and five bags of sand and six bags of sugar weigh 24kg (53lb), how much does each individual bag weigh?

**15** When the grid is complete, no shape will appear more than once in any row or column. Which group of shapes completes the grid – **A**, **B**, **C** or **D**?

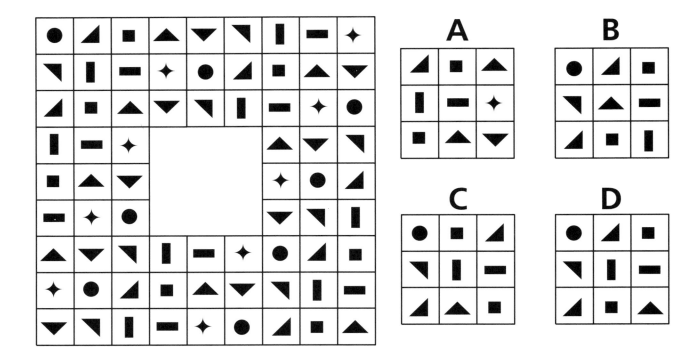

**16** Can you use the logic behind the first flower to complete the second?

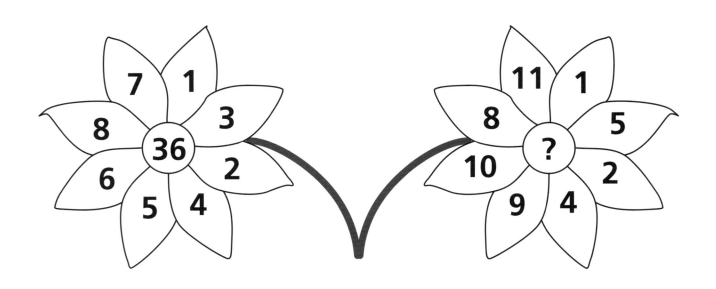

**17** Which shape continues the series – **A**, **B** or **C**?

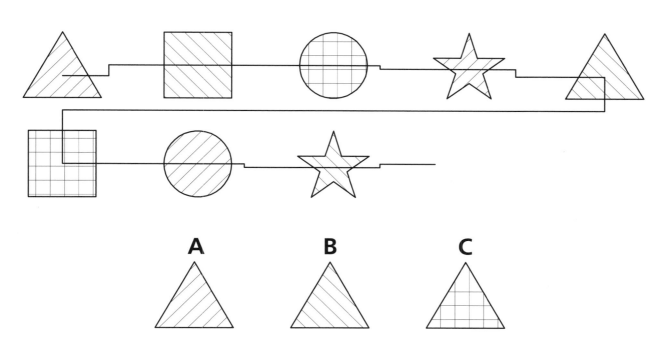

**A**  **B**  **C**

**18** What number should replace the question mark?

| 6 | 16 | 12 | 10 | 18 |
|---|----|----|----|----|
| 48 | 28 | 36 | 40 | ? |

**19** Which dial comes next in the series– **A**, **B**, **C** or **D**?

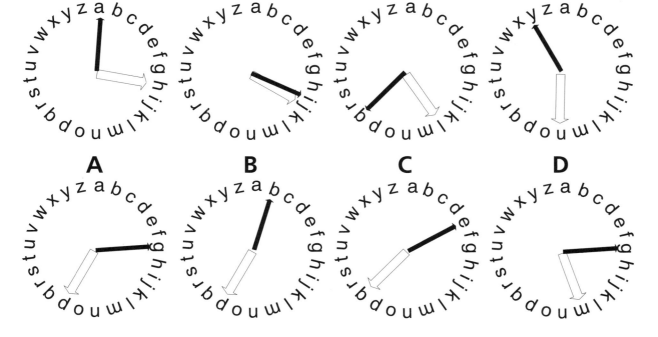

**A**  **B**  **C**  **D**

**20** What number replaces the question mark?

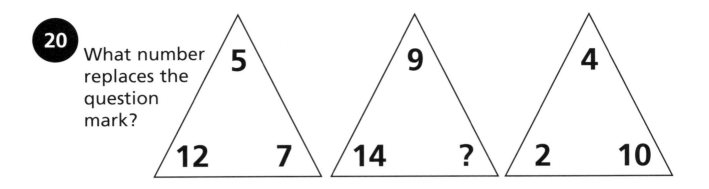

**21** What number comes next in the series?

**22** Can you assign numerical values (all whole numbers lower than 10) to the shapes □, △ and ◯ so that the see-saws are perfectly balanced? You should then be able to work out what replaces the question mark – **A**, **B** or **C**.

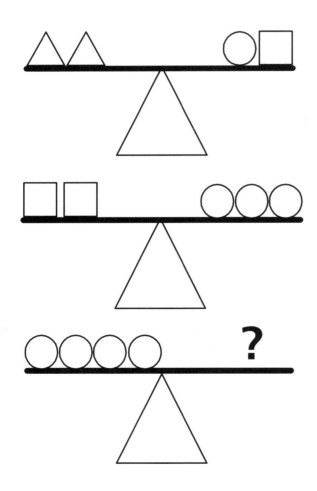

**A**

**B**

**C**

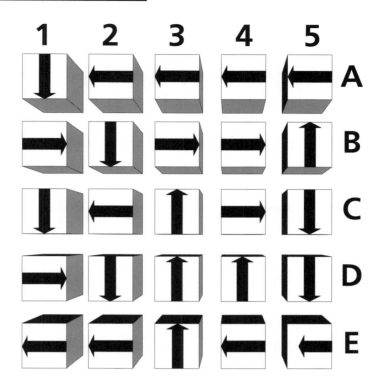

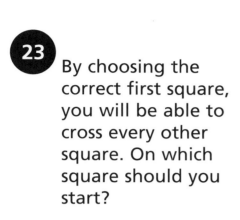

**23** By choosing the correct first square, you will be able to cross every other square. On which square should you start?

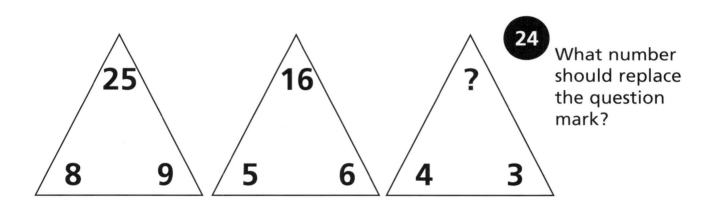

**24** What number should replace the question mark?

**25** Can you find a seven-letter word that includes only the following four letters?

# A B R Y

**26** In how many ways can you read the word TABLE in the grid below? You can read in any direction – horizontally, vertically or diagonally, backwards or forwards, but always in a straight line.

```
B E T L B L B L E E T
L A A E T L L B E
E T L A B B T A L
A E L B A T E L E
T L T T A B L E L
A B B A E L B A T
B A L B B B A B A
L T E L B L L A T
E L A E L B E E L
```

**1** Can you use the logic behind the first flower to complete the second?

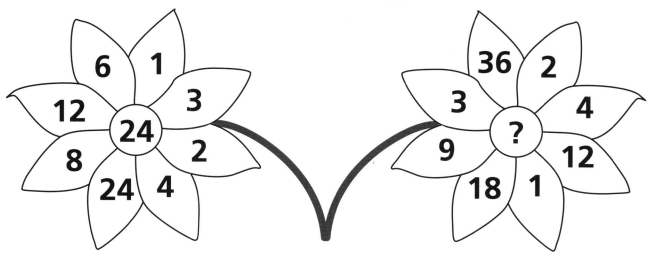

**2** What message is there in the box left?

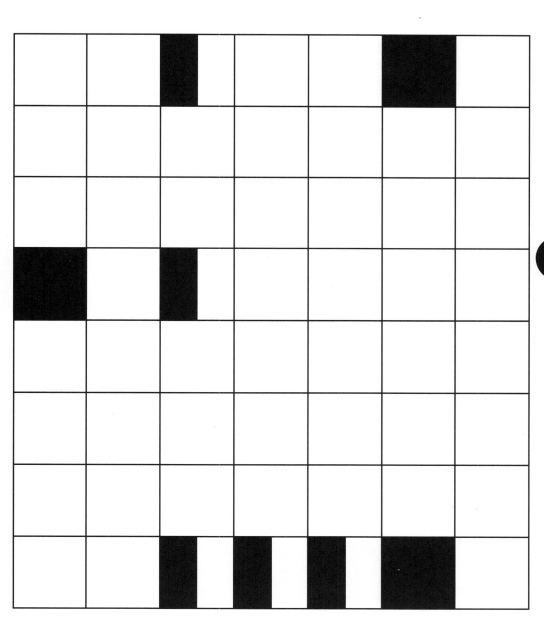

# : LEVEL **12** :

## 825:30

**3** Can you work out which pair or pairs of numbers below have the same relationship to each other as the two numbers above?

417:21    613:17

836:24    928:56

529:25    846:24

**4** Which shape should go into the last triangle – a square or a triangle?

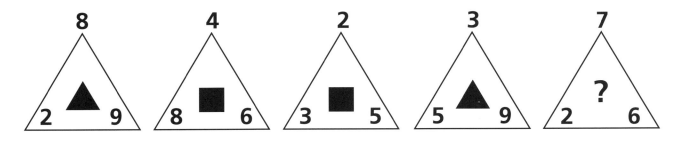

**5** In how many ways can you score 10 points in total with three hoops? Every hoop lands on a hook, and it does not matter in which order they land. It is also possible for more than one hoop to land on any hook.

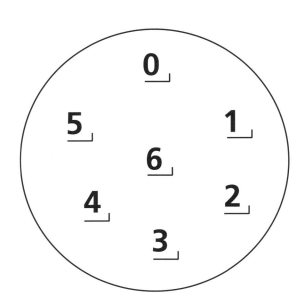

**6**

Can you assign numerical values (all whole numbers lower than 20) to the shapes below so that the see-saws are perfectly balanced? You should then be able to work out what replaces the question mark – **A**, **B** or **C**?

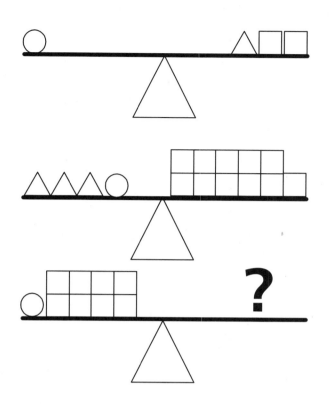

**?**

**A**

**B**

**C**

**7**

What number comes next in the series?

96 — 52 — 30 — 19 — ?

**8**

By choosing the correct first square, you will be able to cross every square. On which square should you start?

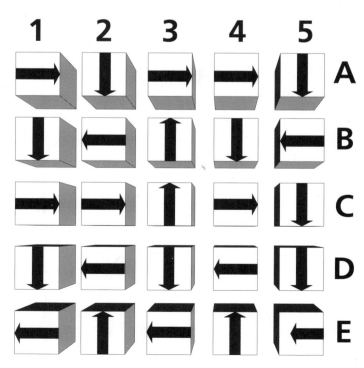

**9** Which dial comes next in the series – **A**, **B C** or **D**?

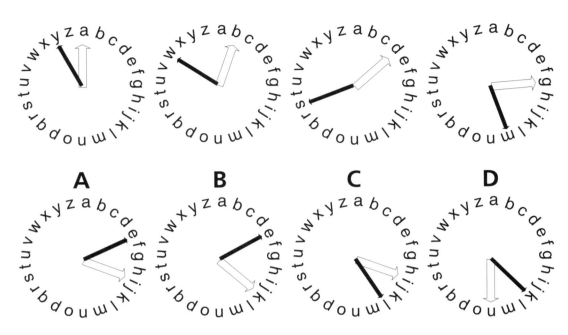

A    B    C    D

**10** See how quickly you can rearrange the letters of the following names so that they spell the job that each individual has?

1. Colin  Meap
2. Ian  Elctrice
3. Sid  Shearrer
4. Ben  Kar
5. Reg  Snide
6. Joan  Lustir
7. Ken  Drurate
8. Mel  Nassa
9. Fred  Augil
10. Ann  Coucatt

**11** Jim Peters lives at 11 Enigma Road; Paul Jones lives at 9 Enigma Road; and Harry Smith lives at 15 Enigma Road. Can you determine with which of them a certain Jessica Clark is living? There is logic you can follow in the information given.

**12** Take a look at this fantasy dartboard, in which you score points according to the rings in which your darts land. Can you work out which rings the darts should land on, to achieve a score of 125, if you throw 6 darts and 4 of them land in just one of the rings?

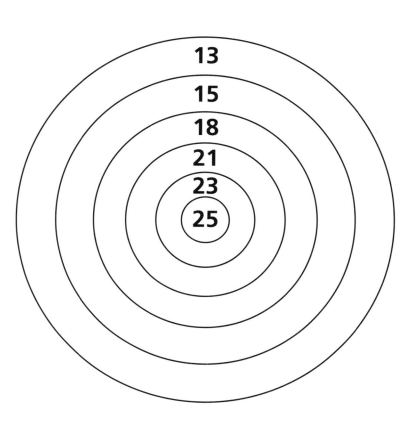

**13** Can you find the odd one out?
Is it **A**, **B C**, **D** or **E**?

| A | B | C | D | E |
|---|---|---|---|---|
| 1225 | 1936 | 1849 | 1972 | 2025 |

# : LEVEL **12** :

**14** Can you find the shortest route to the black square?

**15** Can you rearrange these boxes to form three nine-letter words?

| POR | TRY | ORM |
| --- | --- | --- |
| QUE | TEM | NSF |
| ARY | MAR | TRA |

**16** What number should replace the question mark?

8　6　4

?　11　1

7　5　3

**17** What number replaces the question mark?

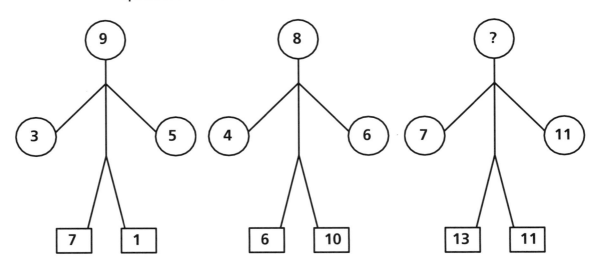

**18** What number should replace the question mark?

| 3 | 5 | 6 | 8 | ? |
|---|---|---|---|---|
| 4 | 8 | 10 | 14 | 18 |

**19** What comes next – **A**, **B** or **C**?

**A**  **B**  **C**

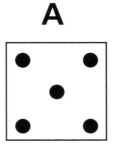 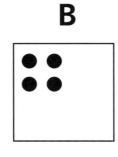 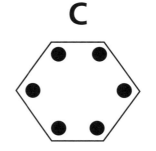

**20** What links the outer numbers to the inner one?

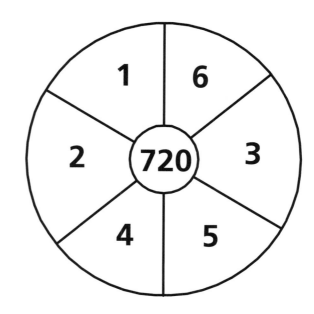

**21** What number replaces the question mark?

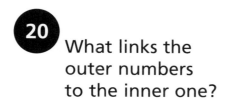

26
5    8

18
3    6

22
5    ?

**22** Which shape fits the hole – **A**, **B**, **C** or **D**? Pieces may be rotated but not flipped over.

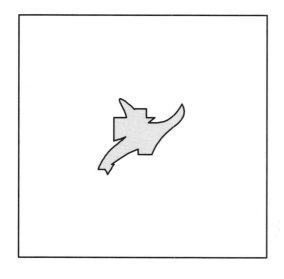

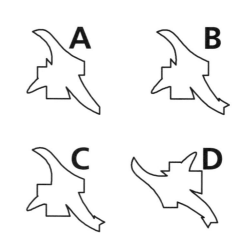

**23** Insert addition, multiplication, division or subtraction signs to make this sum correct.

# 1280 ? 39 ? 5 ? 8 = 399,320

| 1 | 2 | 3 | 4 | 5 | 6 |
|---|---|---|---|---|---|
| A | B | C | D | E | F |
| G | H | I | J | K | L |
| M | N | O | P | Q | R |
| S | T | U | V | W | X |
| Y | Z |   |   |   |   |

**24** Use the table to find the name of a river.

| 3 | 6 | 3 | 2 | 3 | 3 | 3 |
|---|---|---|---|---|---|---|
|   |   |   |   |   |   |   |

**25** What number should replace the question mark?

**1** What letter should replaces the question mark?

# GSOG?

**2** Place 7 coins according to the pattern shown. Can you now move only 2 of them so 5 are left in both the horizontal row and the vertical column?

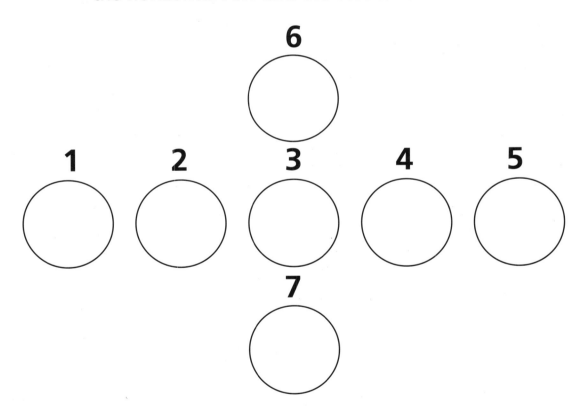

**3** Which is the odd one out? Is it **A**, **B**, **C**, **D** or **E**?

| A | B | C | D | E |
|---|---|---|---|---|
| 1649 | 2581 | 1634 | 6409 | 4904 |

**4** In Farmer Brown's field in Australia, there are both ostriches and cows. If there are 82 creatures in all and 244 legs, how many ostriches are there?

**5** Can you work out which numbers should go in the empty spaces? In each instance, the same logic is used, from the top and working clockwise.

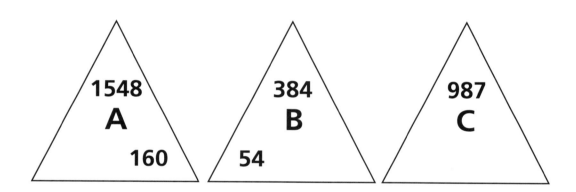

**6** What number comes next in the series?

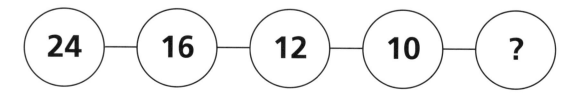

**7** Can you use the logic behind the first flower to complete the second? The answer is a single figure.

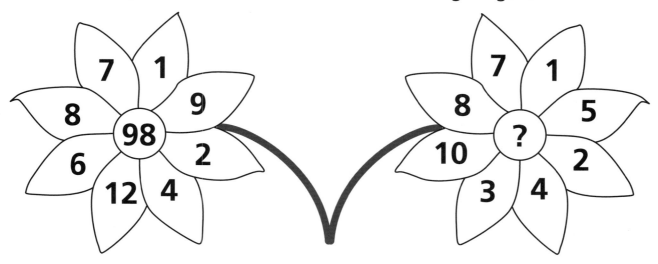

**8** What number will complete the grid?

| 0 | 1 | 4 | 9 |
|---|---|---|---|
| 121 | 144 | 169 | 16 |
| 100 | ? | 196 | 25 |
| 81 | 64 | 49 | 36 |

**9** Can you rearrange these boxes to form three nine-letter words?

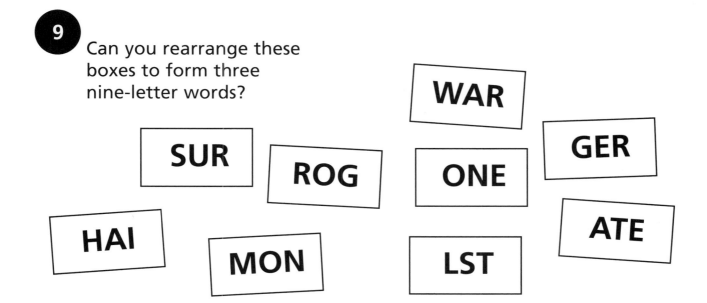

**10** A canoeist decides to paddle up river, go around a buoy and return to base without leaving the river. The buoy is 16km upstream. Each day, he rows for 12 hours, covering 3km per day.

He then sleeps for 12 hours always. But while he is asleep, the river's constant current washes him back 2km downstream. Assuming he will start his return journey the instant he reaches the buoy, how long will it take him to complete the circuit?

**11** Can you arrange the above blocks to form a magic square? (A magic square is, of course, a square in which the horizontal rows, vertical columns and diagonals all add up to the same number.) There are a number of ways to do this.

| 6 | 12 |
|---|----|
| 15 | 1 |

| 3 | 13 |
|---|----|
| 10 | 8 |

| 9 | 7 |
|---|----|
| 4 | 14 |

| 16 | 2 |
|----|---|
| 5 | 11 |

**12** Can you draw this letter without taking your pen off the paper and in one continuous line?

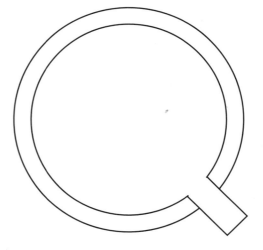

**13** Can you put the correct mathematical symbols into the spaces to make the sum correct?

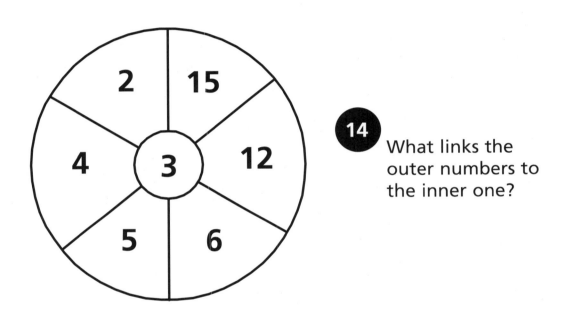

8  6  7  5  =  105

**14** What links the outer numbers to the inner one?

2   15

4   **3**   12

5   6

**15** Can you read this message?

U J I K T U M O T

T O D H H T E T E

T H L P H N E L S

U E I E T A M E M

**16** Which box differs in one respect from all the rest?

A B C

D E F

G H I

**17** Use the table to find the name of a famous European battle.

| 1 | 2 | 3 | 4 | 5 | 6 |
|---|---|---|---|---|---|
| A | B | C | D | E | F |
| G | H | I | J | K | L |
| M | N | O | P | Q | R |
| S | T | U | V | W | X |
| Y | Z | | | | |

| 1 | 1 | 3 | 2 | 3 | 3 | 3 | 6 | 2 |
|---|---|---|---|---|---|---|---|---|
| | | | | | | | | |

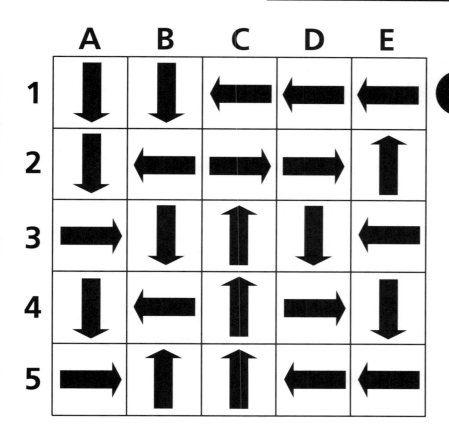

**18** By choosing one arrow and following the succeeding arrows, you should be able to travel through 24 of the 25 boxes. Which is the unused arrow, which is the final arrow, and with which arrow should you have started?

**19** The faces in the grid form a logical patters. Which group completes the grid – **A**, **B** or **C**?

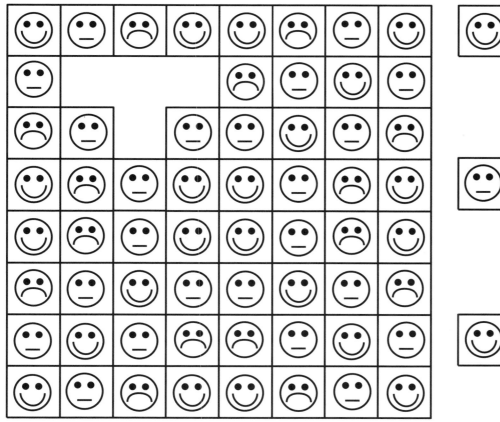

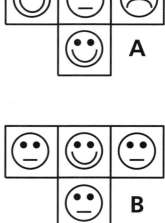

**20** What number replaces the question mark?

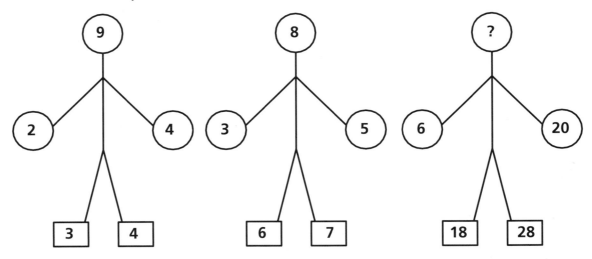

| 40 | 24 | 16 | 32 | 4 |
|----|----|----|----|---|
| 11 | 7  | 5  | 9  | ? |

**21** What number should replace the question mark?

**22** Which shape fits the hole – **A**, **B**, **C** or **D**?

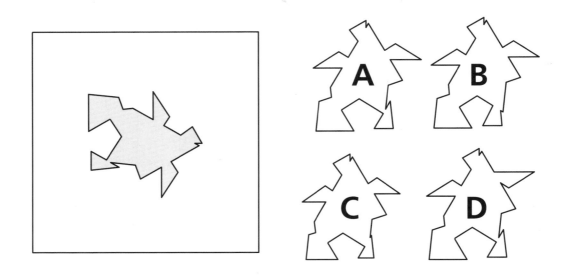

**23** If you were given three large, solid wooden blocks of equal size and a piece of string, and then asked if you could cut the string to a length equal to the distance between the two most distant corners on a block (**A & B**), how could you complete the task?

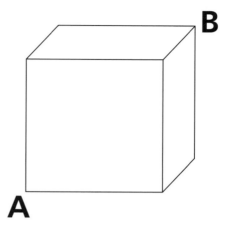

**24** Which dial comes next in this series – **A**, **B**, **C** or **D**?

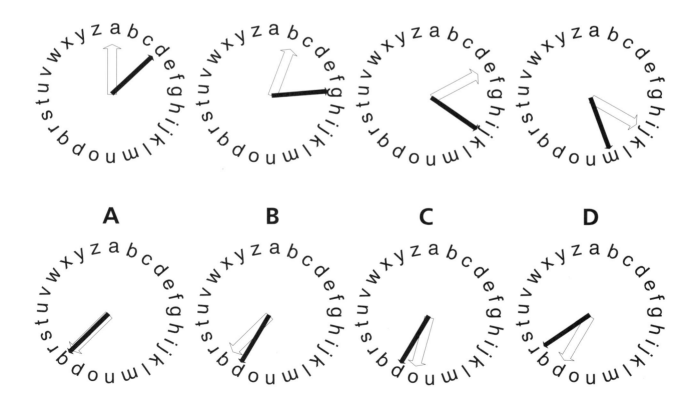

**A**          **B**          **C**          **D**

**25** Which letter do these pieces make when rearranged?

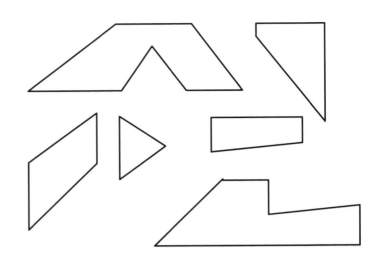

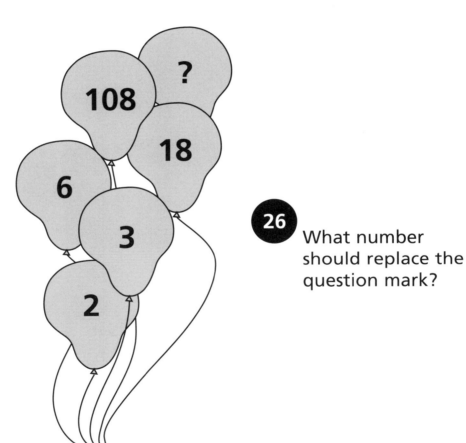

**26** What number should replace the question mark?

**27** Two cyberpets cost the same as 5 yo-yos, 3 yo-yos cost the same as 60 marbles, and marbles are priced at 10 for $1. If a boy swaps his cyberpet for $6 cash, is this a good bargain?

**1** Which box differs in one respect from all the rest?

A

B

C

D

E

F

G

H

I

**2** Which dial comes next in the series – **A, B, C** or **D**?

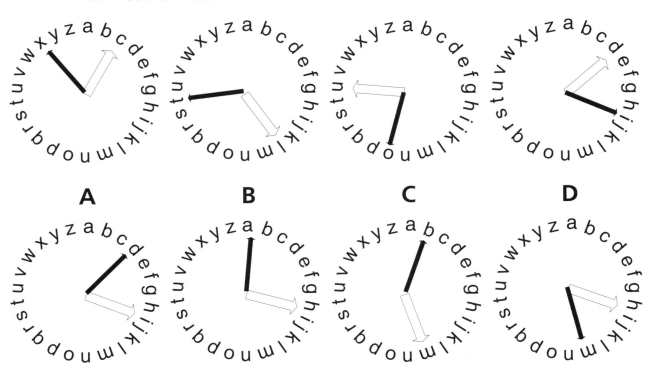

**A**        **B**        **C**        **D**

**3** How many minutes is it past 10 a.m. now if, 45 minutes ago, it was 4 times as many minutes past 9 a.m?

**4** Can you think of a 5-letter word that comprises only the following letters?

# NOI

**5** Can you use the logic behind the first flower to complete the second?

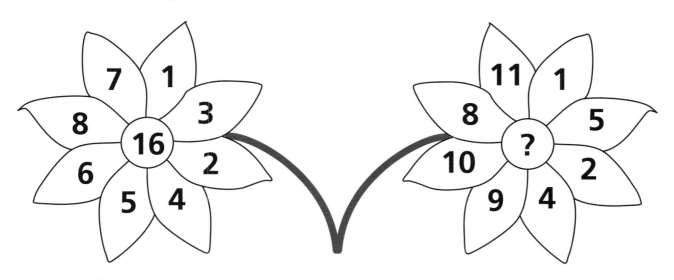

**6** Use the shapes shown on the grid to complete it. Once complete, no horizontal row or vertical column should contain two similar shapes. Which shape therefore replaces the question mark?

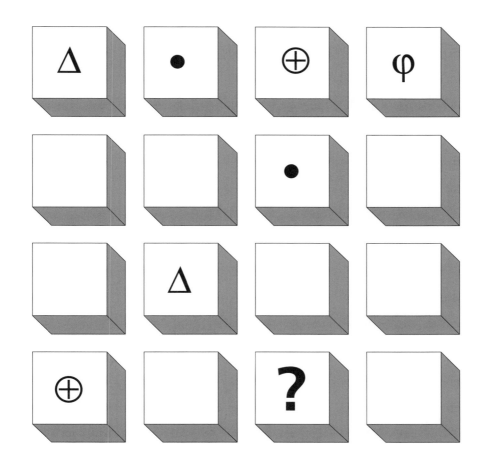

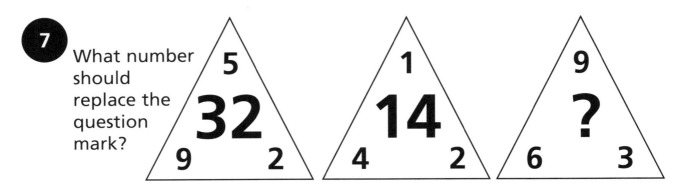

**7** What number should replace the question mark?

5 / 32 / 9 2

1 / 14 / 4 2

9 / ? / 6 3

**8** Lay out 6 matches to form the pattern shown. Can you now move 2 of them and then add one more so that you will then have 2 diamond shapes?

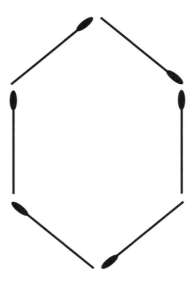

**9** Can you find the odd one out?

**A**
2460

**B**
3251

**C**
6152

**D**
1836

**E**
2204

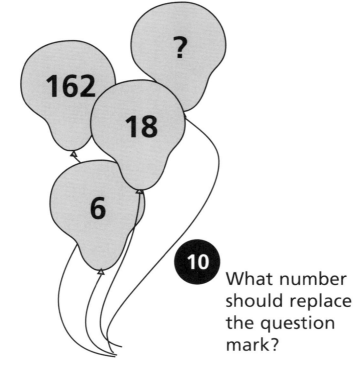

162

18

6

?

**10** What number should replace the question mark?

**11** What number replaces the question mark?

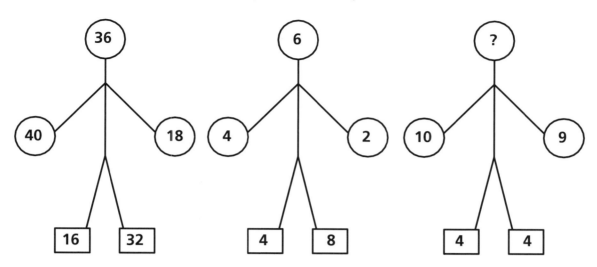

| A | B | D | G |

| P | N | K | G |

**12** Which letter continues the top series?
And which letter continues the bottom series?

**13** What number replaces the question mark?

| 7 | 9 | 5 | 6 | 8 |
|---|---|---|---|---|
| 23 | 31 | 15 | 19 | ? |

**14** Which letter do these pieces form when rearranged?

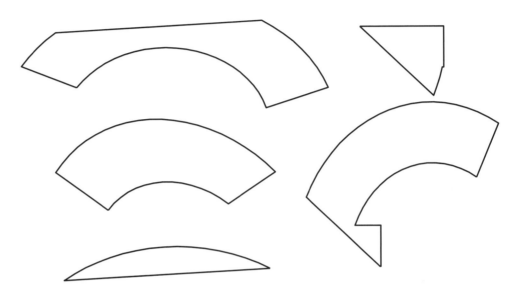

**15** Which number completes this grid?

| 0 | 66 | 55 | 45 |
|---|----|----|----|
| 1 | 78 | ? | 36 |
| 3 | 91 | 105 | 28 |
| 6 | 10 | 15 | 21 |

**16** Gillian is half as old again as Paul, and he is 28 years older than Mary.

If their combined ages total 161, how old is each of them?

**17**

Which of the following is not
an anagram of an animal?

## 1. TONE PLEA    4. RASH MET
## 2. BED RAG      5. COAL PET
## 3. PROBS KING   6. RAIN AGENT

**18**

By choosing the correct block as a starting point, you will be
able to cross all 25 blocks. With which block should you begin?

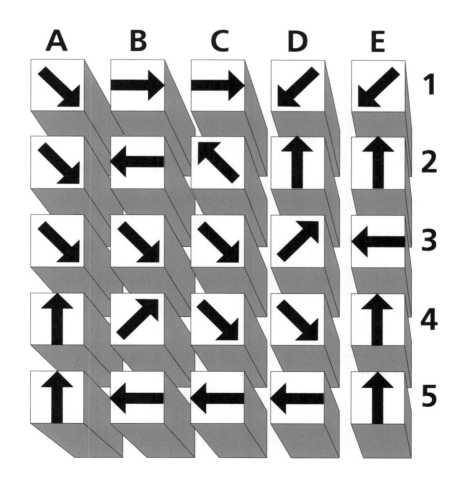

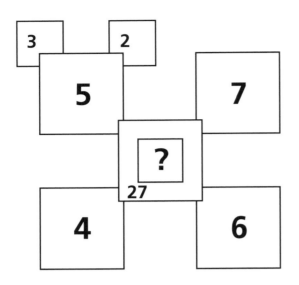

**19** Which number logically fits on the top platform?

**20** Can you rearrange these boxes to form three nine-letter words?

| ION | ATT | EQU |
|-----|-----|-----|
| ONS | ATI | TER |
| ENT | RAP | INS |

| 1 | 2 | 3 | 4 | 5 |
|---|---|---|---|---|
| A | B | C | D | E |
| F | G | H | I | J |
| K | L | M | N | O |
| P | Q | R | S | T |
| U | V | W | X | Y |

**21** Use the table to find the name of a famous car.

| 2 | 1 | 3 | 2 | 5 | 3 | 2 | 3 | 4 | 4 | 4 |
|---|---|---|---|---|---|---|---|---|---|---|
|   |   |   |   |   |   |   |   |   |   |   |

**22** Which shape fits the hole – **A**, **B**, **C** or **D**?

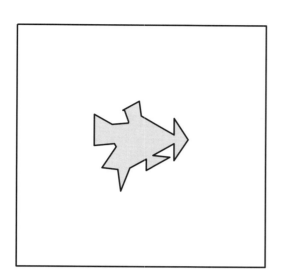

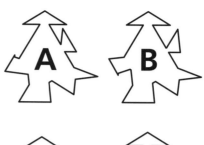

**23** What links the outer numbers to the inner one?

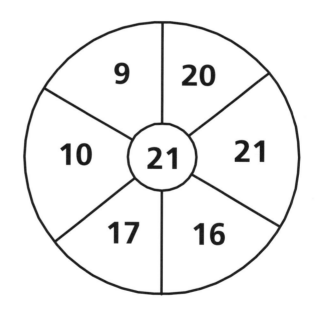

**24** What number should fill the blank space?

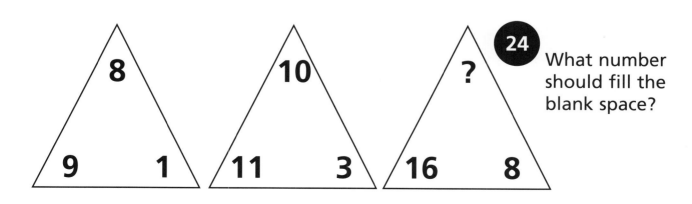

**25** Which one-digit number replaces the question mark?

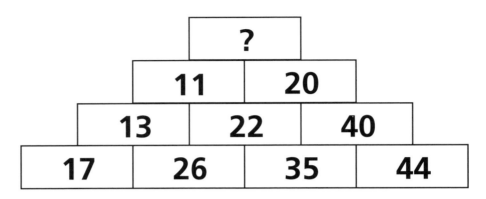

**26** While inspecting some graffiti on the wall of the school gymnasium, Mr Addy had to admit that the Academy for Gentlemen, of which he was headmaster, provided a better class of vandal; even the graffiti was of an educational quality. It read as follows:

$$99 \div 9 = 11$$

Grabbing an unfortunate student by the ear, Mr Addy said: "Ah, young Smythe, how would you like to do a spot of cleaning?"

Upon the boy's understandable protestation, Mr Addy continued: "All right, I'll make a bargain with you. If you can tell me which mathematical symbols the vandal could have added to the same sum to make the answer come to two without changing any of the figures in the sum, I'll let you off."

Unfortunately for Smythe, maths was not his strongest subject and he ended up scrubbing the wall.

**Looking at the above sum, can you see which two mathematical symbols could indeed be added to 99÷9 to make the resulting answer equal 2?**

**1**

Once, long ago, a blind, old witch employed men, one by one, to work her goldmine. Instead of payment, however, she struck a bargain with them. If they worked hard and never tried to cheat her, they could keep half of all the gold they could mine in a day. If she caught them trying to swindle her, though, they would instantly turn to stone. So far, not one had been honest, and her grounds were therefore littered, quite literally, with grotesque statues.

To help her with her surveillance of the task, the witch had three magic talking sacks which understood English and which were used for holding the gold. She would ask her magic sacks how much gold each of them had held that day on the way back from the mine, and it was then that she would discover any fraud.

When an honest man named Simon did finally apply for the job, he agreed to the witch's terms but added that, if she should ever wrongly accuse him of theft, *she* would turn to stone instead of him. The witch, who had grown conceited over the years, promptly agreed.

One night, however, he happened to hear her talking sacks and promptly devised a plan both to rid the world of the witch and to take over the mine. The next day, Simon handed the witch eight ounces of gold, kept the rest, and returned the empty sacks. That night, the witch could hardly wait for Simon to fall asleep. She then snatched up the sacks and asked them, as always, how much gold they had each held that day.

"I held one ounce," whispered the first sack.

"I held two ounces," whispered the second sack.

"I held sixteen ounces," whispered the third.

The witch could hardly contain herself.

Quickly, she fumbled her way to Simon's quarters. "Wake up you thief, you scoundrel, you fool!" she screamed.

"What are you saying?" Simon asked.

"I am saying that you are just like all the rest. Thief, prepare to meet thy doom!"

The witch's screams of satisfaction were short-lived, however, and soon turned to shrieks of horror as *she* slowly began to turn to stone. Moments later, she was just another hideous statue. Simon then took his pick and smashed her to dust.

How had Simon succeeded in outwitting the witch?

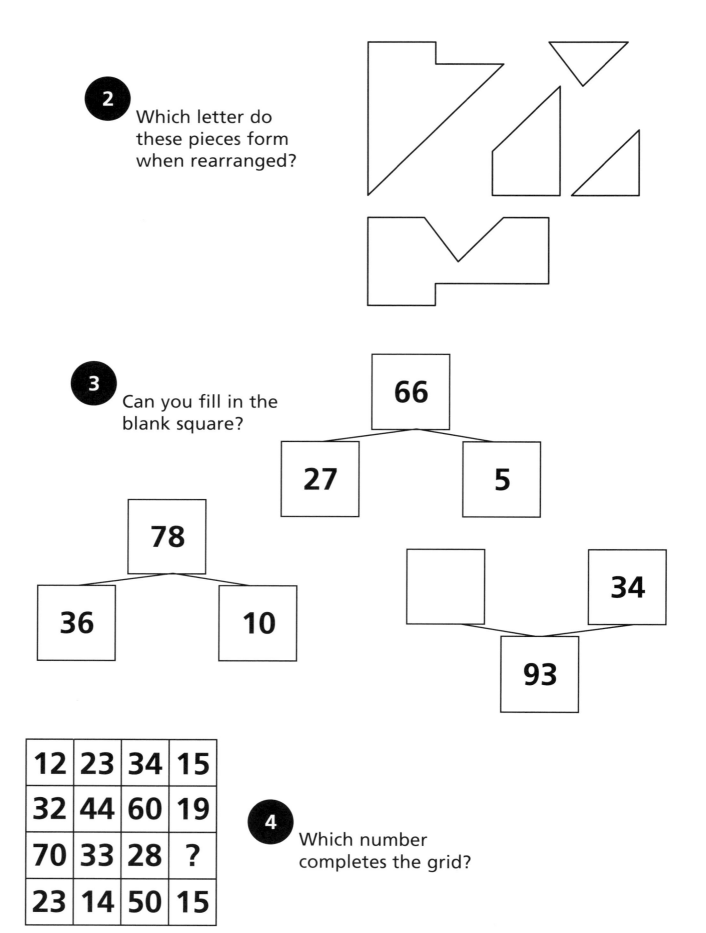

**2** Which letter do these pieces form when rearranged?

**3** Can you fill in the blank square?

66

27    5

78

36    10

34

93

| 12 | 23 | 34 | 15 |
|----|----|----|----|
| 32 | 44 | 60 | 19 |
| 70 | 33 | 28 | ? |
| 23 | 14 | 50 | 15 |

**4** Which number completes the grid?

**5** What number should replace the question mark?

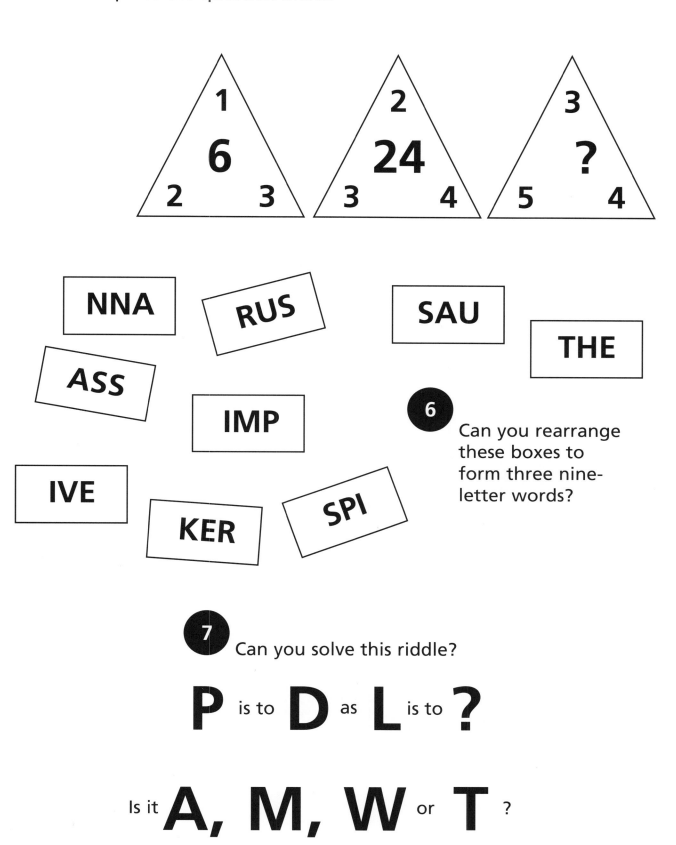

Triangle 1: 1, 6, 2, 3

Triangle 2: 2, 24, 3, 4

Triangle 3: 3, ?, 5, 4

NNA   RUS   SAU   THE

ASS   IMP   IVE   KER   SPI

**6** Can you rearrange these boxes to form three nine-letter words?

**7** Can you solve this riddle?

P is to D as L is to ?

Is it A, M, W or T ?

**8** Can you insert all the numbers given so that each horizontal row, vertical column and diagonal adds up to 18?
1, 1, 2, 3, 3, 4, 4, 4, 5, 6, 7, 8.

| | | | 6 |
|---|---|---|---|
| 2 | | | |
| | | 9 | |
| | 7 | | |

**9** What letter comes next in this line?

# MVEMJ?

| 12 | 5 | 15 | 17 | 20 |
|---|---|---|---|---|
| 19 | 27 | 16 | 15 | ? |

**10** What number should replace the question mark?

**11** Long ago, a king built a fortress containing 64 square towers arranged as the diagram shows, the towers all being connected by a system of bridges.

One night, the king set out to walk from his tower (the grey tower) to his wife's tower (the black tower). On his way, he passed through every other tower and made his journey in exactly fifteen straight lines.

**Can you work out the route that the king took?**

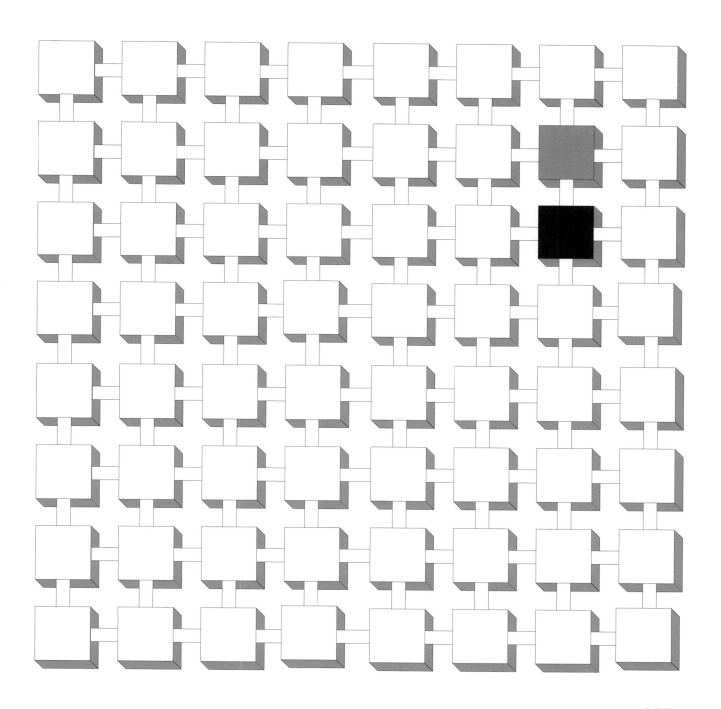

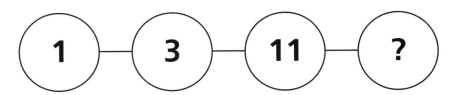

**12** What number comes next in this series?

( 1 ) — ( 3 ) — ( 11 ) — ( ? )

△7 □4 ○2 △3

□8 ○? △2 □4

○8 △9 □5 ○6

**13** What number should replace the question mark?

**14** Can you use the tables below to find the name of a famous boxer?

| 3 | 5 | 3 | 1 | 5 |
|---|---|---|---|---|
|   |   |   |   |   |

| 3 | 1 | 3 | 3 | 4 | 1 | 4 | 5 |
|---|---|---|---|---|---|---|---|
|   |   |   |   |   |   |   |   |

| 1 | 2 | 3 | 4 | 5 |
|---|---|---|---|---|
| A | B | C | D | E |
| F | G | H | I | J |
| K | L | M | N | O |
| P | Q | R | S | T |
| U | V | W | X | Y |

**15** What number completes the grid?

| 1 | 3 | 4 | 12 |
|---|---|---|----|
| 2 | 3 | 2 | 12 |
| 3 | 4 | 5 | 60 |
| 4 | 3 | 4 | ? |

**16** What links the
outer numbers to
the inner one?

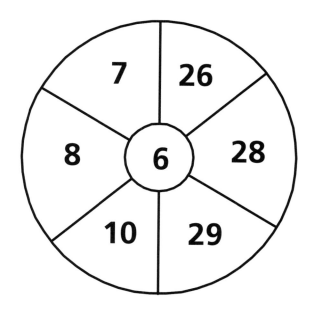

**17** When Avril organised a picnic, she brought
along melons she thought would be thirst-
quenching. They got through half of them,
plus half a melon, and were left with one
whole melon. How many had Avril provided
for the picnic to start with?

**18** Which shape fits the hole – **A**, **B**, **C** or **D**?

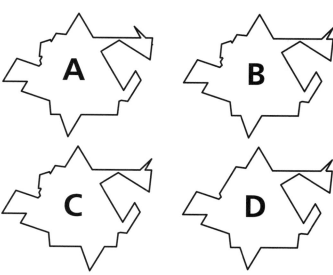

**19** Which dial comes next in the series – **A**, **B**, **C** or **D**?

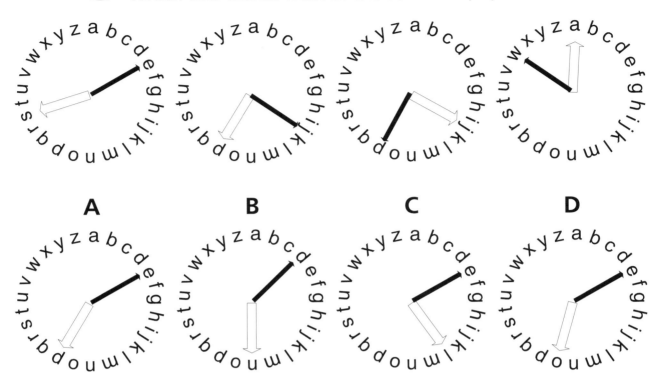

**A**     **B**     **C**     **D**

**20** It was most unfortunate. When everyone had arrived at the opening of the flower-show by Lady Forsythe at 2.30pm, it was bright and sunny.

But just a quarter-of-an-hour later, the heavens opened with the result that only the most enthusiastic of visitors, and those with umbrellas, stayed on.

At 3pm, one quarter left; and half-an-hour later, one-fifth of those then remaining left, too.

At 4pm, three-quarters of those then left departed as well, so that only 33 were still there to enjoy strawberries and cream in the tea tent.

**How many visitors had been present when the flower-show was declared open at 2.30pm?**

**21** Which grid comes next in the series – **A**, **B**, **C** or **D**?

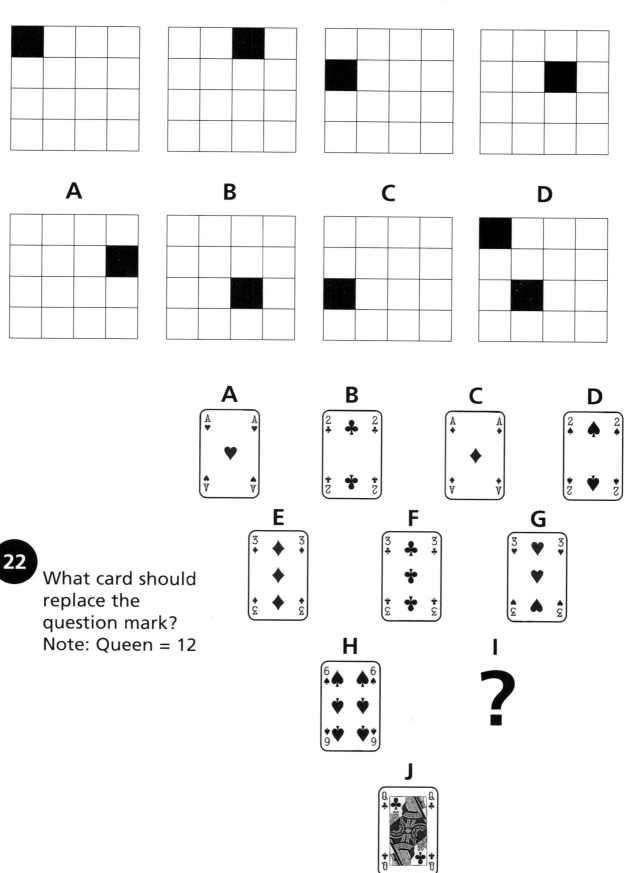

**A**  **B**  **C**  **D**

**A**  **B**  **C**  **D**

**E**  **F**  **G**

**22** What card should replace the question mark?
Note: Queen = 12

**H**

**I**

**?**

**J**

# LEVEL 15

**23** Which of the shields shown should be placed in the blank space – **A, B, C** or **D**?

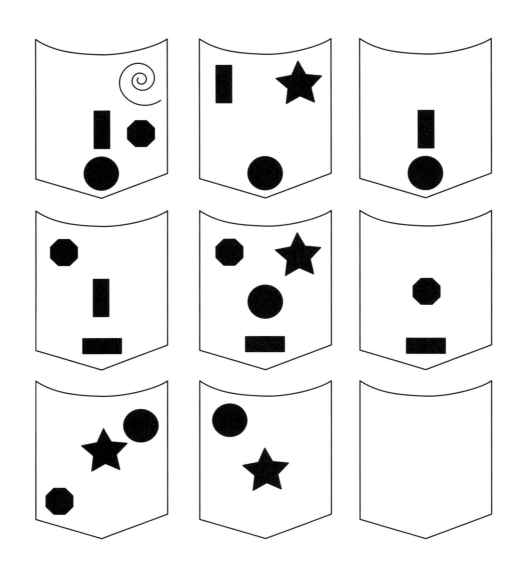

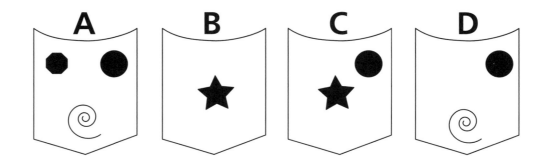

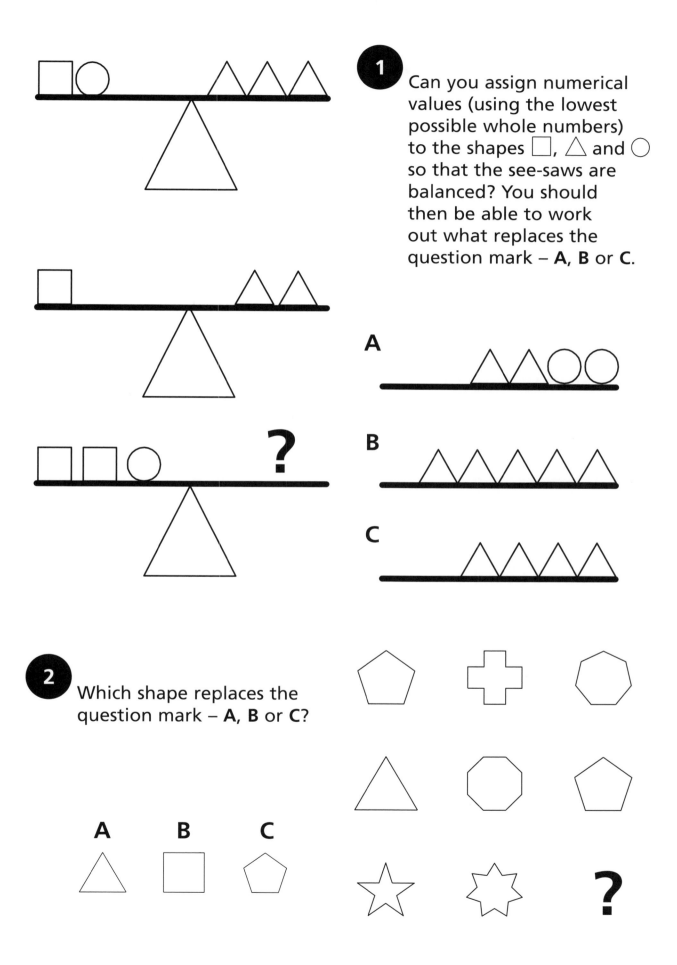

**1** Can you assign numerical values (using the lowest possible whole numbers) to the shapes □, △ and ○ so that the see-saws are balanced? You should then be able to work out what replaces the question mark – **A**, **B** or **C**.

**A**

**B**

**C**

**2** Which shape replaces the question mark – **A**, **B** or **C**?

**A** **B** **C**

**3** Which dial comes next in the series – **A**, **B**, **C** or **D**?

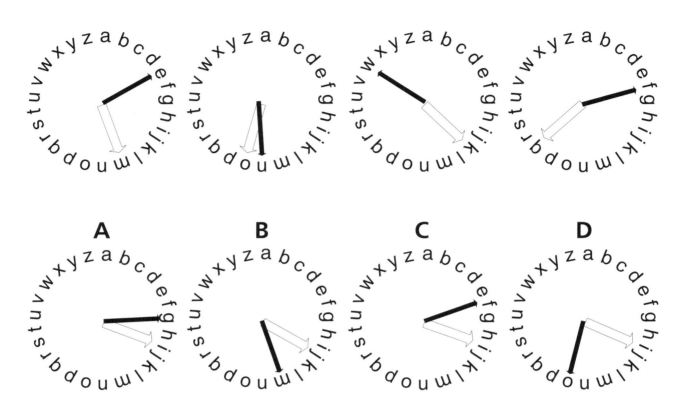

**A**        **B**        **C**        **D**

**4** One day, a couple arrived at a carpenter's workshop. They had with them a fine table, the top of which measured 1m square and was made from 4 separate panels joined together, the sides of each panel measuring 50cm (20in).

The couple told the carpenter they wanted a similar table. Again, the four sides of the top were each to measure 1m (40in), but this time it was to be made of 8 panels, each side of every panel being 50cm (20in) in length.

At first, the only way the carpenter could see of producing the new table was to make the top twice as thick. The couple went on to explain, however, the way in which their request could be fulfilled so that the tabletop would be just one layer thick.

**Can you design this tabletop?**

**5** Can you use the logic behind the first flower to complete the second?

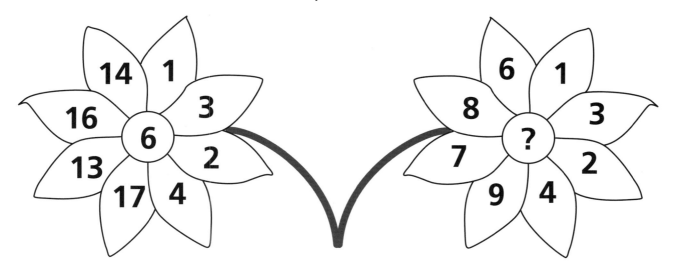

**6** Can you rearrange these boxes to form three nine-letter words?

| CAL | IST | PTI |
|-----|-----|-----|
| LIS | REA | TIC |
| ICE | ARM | SKE |

| 1 | 2 | 3 | 4 | 5 |
|---|---|---|---|---|
| A | B | C | D | E |
| F | G | H | I | J |
| K | L | M | N | O |
| P | Q | R | S | T |
| U | V | W | X | Y |

**7** Can you use the tables to find the name of a type of pasta?

| 5 | 1 | 2 | 2 | 4 | 1 | 5 | 5 | 2 | 2 | 5 |
|---|---|---|---|---|---|---|---|---|---|---|
|   |   |   |   |   |   |   |   |   |   |   |

**8** Which box differs in one respect from all the rest?

A   B   C

D   E   F

G   H   I

**9** What number replaces the question mark?

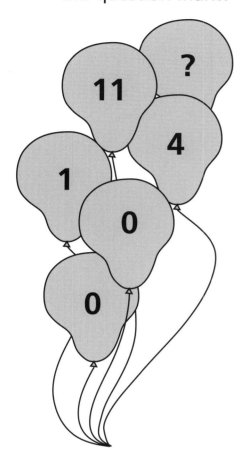

**10** Which letter do these pieces form when rearranged?

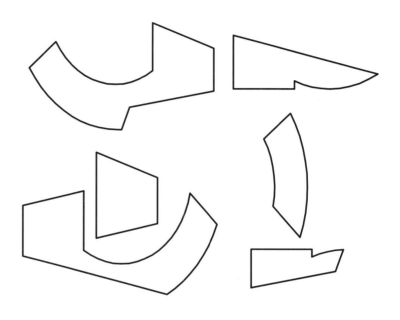

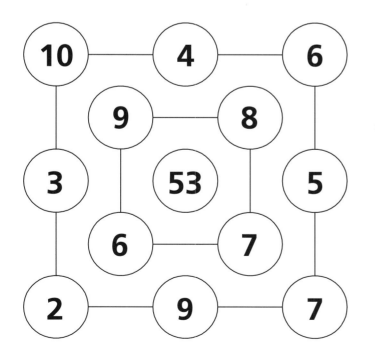

**11** What links the centre circle to the surrounding circles?

| 12 | 40 | 71 | 51 | 56 |
|----|----|----|----|----|
| 90 | 44 | 22 | 33 | ?  |

**12** What number should replace the question mark?

**13** What number should fill the blank space?

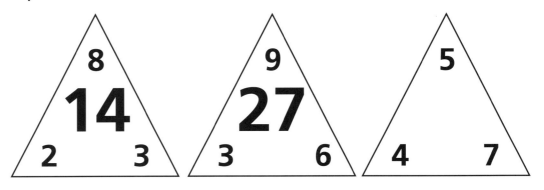

**14** Which domino (A, B, C, D or E) should fill the empty space?

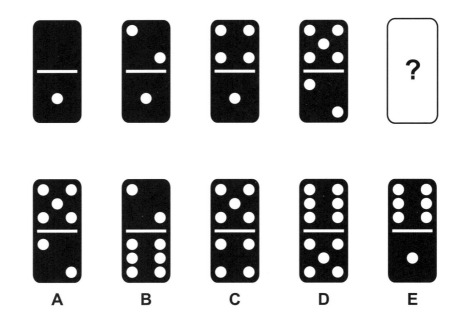

A    B    C    D    E

**15** What letter should fill the blank space?

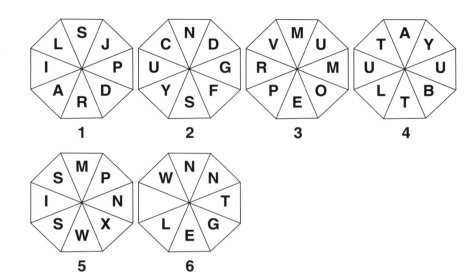

**16** What number should replace the question mark?

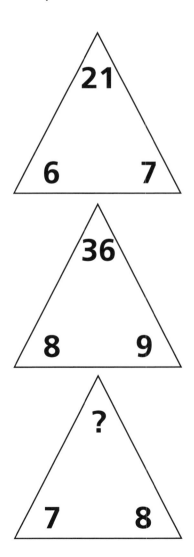

**17** What letter should replace the question mark?

| A | B | C | D | E |
|---|---|---|---|---|
| B | D | E | F | D |
| C | E | F | E | C |
| D | F | E | ? | B |
| E | D | C | B | A |

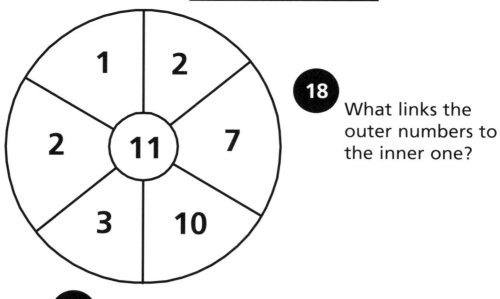

**18** What links the outer numbers to the inner one?

**19** What number replaces the question mark?

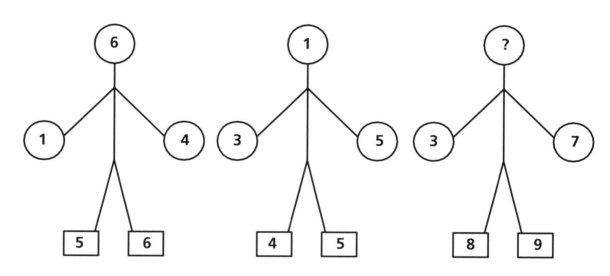

**20** Which shape fits the hole – **A**, **B**, **C** or **D**?

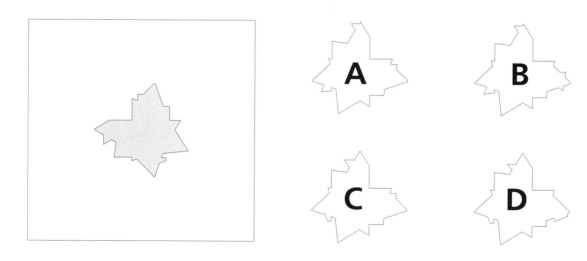

**21** When this shape is folded to make a box, which of the following arrangements can be created – **A**, **B**, **C** or **D**?

**A**

**B**

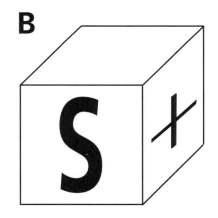

**C**

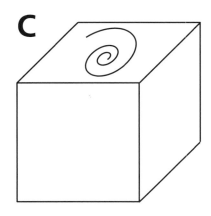

**D**

**22** Which grid comes next in the series – **A**, **B** or **C**?

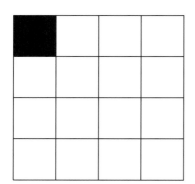
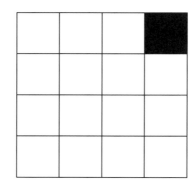
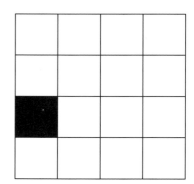

**A**          **B**          **C**

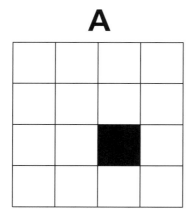
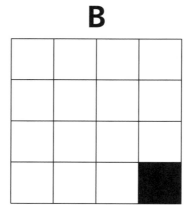
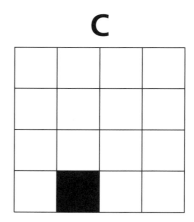

**23** At a family gathering, Douglas was showing a photograph of a man to three uncles he had not seen for several years.

The father of this man, he explained – always one to enjoy a cryptic remark – was 58 years old and was his father's son.

This might seem strange at first because Douglas had no brothers and it was not a grandson.

**So who was in the picture?**

**1** Ten people are dealt cards from the Diamonds and Spades suits only of a pack, the picture cards – Jacks, Queens and Kings – having been removed. Aces are given a value of one in this game.

Each of the ten receives 2 cards. **Can you tell from the following information which cards each of the ten holds?**

- Adele's two cards total 13, the higher one being red and the one of lower value, black.

- Brenda has one black and one red card, and they add up to 5.

- The total of Caroline's cards is 2.

- Derek has two red cards that total 17.

- Evan's cards are red and black, the red one being lower, and both add up to 15.

- Fred's cards total 8.

- Gemma's cards are both black and total 19.

- Harry's cards are both red and total 7.

- Isabel's two cards are red and black, and add up to 12.

- Jasmine's two cards total 12, too.

**2** Which letter lies centrally between J and U and Q and F?

| A | N | F | O | I |
|---|---|---|---|---|
| M | B | S | V | P |
| Q | R | C | H | J |
| L | G | W | D | Y |
| T | X | U | K | E |

**3** Can you arrange 6 matches so that each touches all of the other five? Sounds impossible? It's not!

**4** Which is the odd one out? All are anagrams.

1. TPUEENN
2. RUIJETP
3. NURSTA
4. RHEAT
5. METOC
6. RNASUU

**5** Which letter should replace the question mark?

| ? | 6 | 7 | 1 | U |
|---|---|---|---|---|
| 2 | | | | 8 |
| 3 | | | | 3 |
| 3 | | | | 2 |
| R | 6 | 1 | 6 | X |

**6** Disaster! By accident, Professor Cretaceous' secretary has torn up an important list of prehistoric creatures to be put on exhibit and is trying to piece together the names before retyping it. Can you help her with this task?

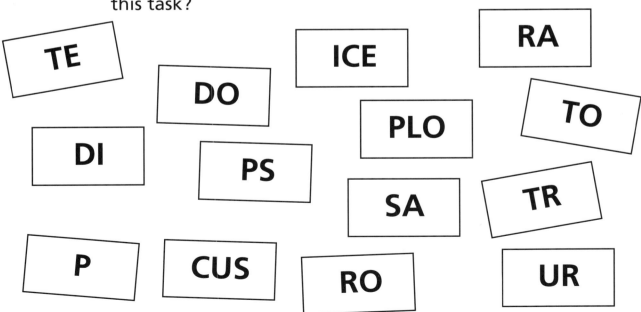

**7** Arrange the numbers 1-16 inclusive, one per square, to complete the equations. Each equation is solved in the order in which the numbers appear, eg the equation 13 + 5 ÷ 2 x 6 = 54 would be solved as 13 + 5 (=18) ÷ 2 (=9) x 6 = 54. Four numbers have been placed to start you off.

|  | + |  | x |  | – | 1 | = | 29 |
| --- | --- | --- | --- | --- | --- | --- | --- | --- |
| + |  | x |  | + |  | x |  |  |
|  | ÷ |  | x | 10 | – |  | = | 13 |
| + |  | + |  | – |  | + |  |  |
|  | + | 15 | – |  | ÷ |  | = | 3 |
| – |  | ÷ |  | + |  | – |  |  |
| 9 | + |  | – |  | + |  | = | 18 |
| = |  | = |  | = |  | = |  |  |
| 15 |  | 4 |  | 23 |  | 2 |  |  |

**8** While in the Negev Desert, a traveller ran out of food supplies but, fortunately, was offered warm hospitality by two Bedhouin.

One of these tribesmen had five flat loaves, freshly baked that morning, and the other had three, also freshly baked.

Both willingly shared the eight loaves among the three of them, each eating no more nor less than any other man. Eternally grateful for this life-saving sustenance, the traveller gave the Bedhouin eight $1 notes.

**How should the two have shared this out?**

**9** Which box differs in one respect from the rest?

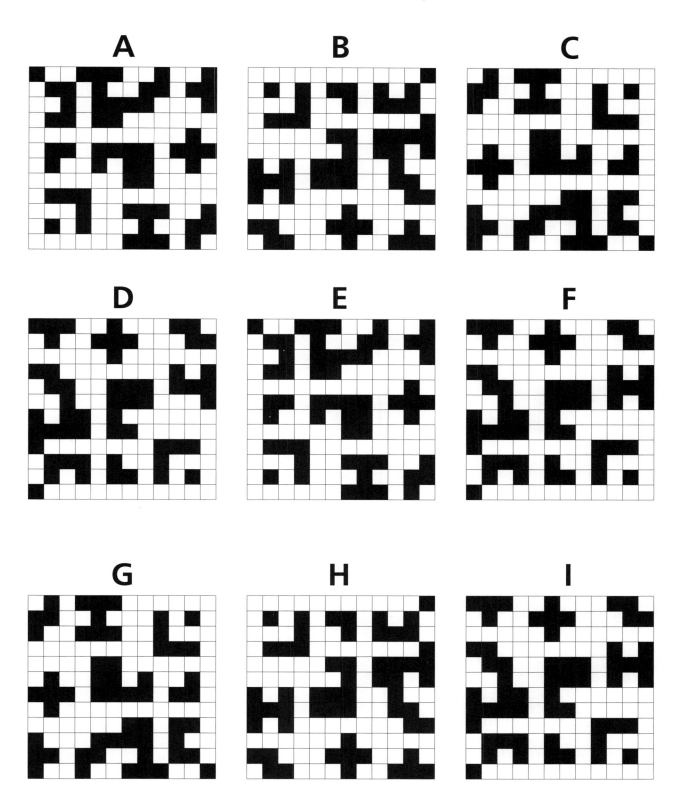

A    B    C

D    E    F

G    H    I

**10** Can you find the shortest route to the exit?

**IN**

**OUT**

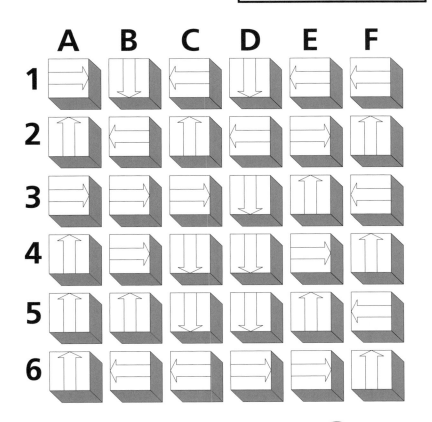

**11** Which square must you start on to be able to cross every square?

**12** Which grid comes next in the series – **A**, **B** or **C**?

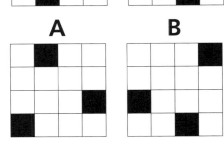

A    B    C

| 1 | 2 | 3 | 4 |
|---|---|---|---|
| A | B | C | D |
| E | F | G | H |
| I | Q | L | M |
| N | O | P | R |
| S | T | U | V |
| W | X | Y | Z |

**13** Can you use the table left to find the name of a former Portuguese colony?

| 4 | 2 | 4 | 1 | 4 | 2 | 1 | 2 | 3 | 1 |
|---|---|---|---|---|---|---|---|---|---|
|   |   |   |   |   |   |   |   |   |   |

**14** From the number given below, what result do you get if you multiply by 7 the total you get by adding together each odd number that appears before an even number?

# 8 3 4 2 1 6 8 9 5 7 4 9 5 3 8

**15** Can you put the following numbers into the grid so that each horizontal row, vertical column and diagonal line of four squares has the same total?

# 0, 1, 2, 2, 2, 3, 4, 6, 7, 7, 7, 9, 13, 15, 17, 17.

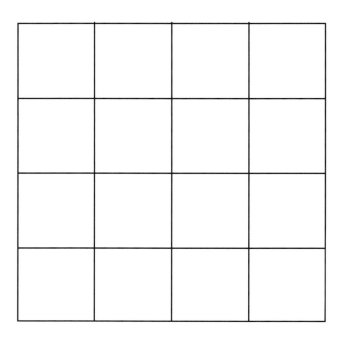

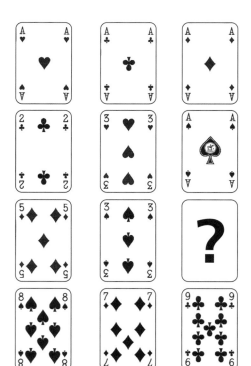

**16** Can you identify the missing card?

**17** Use the logic behind the first flower to complete the second.

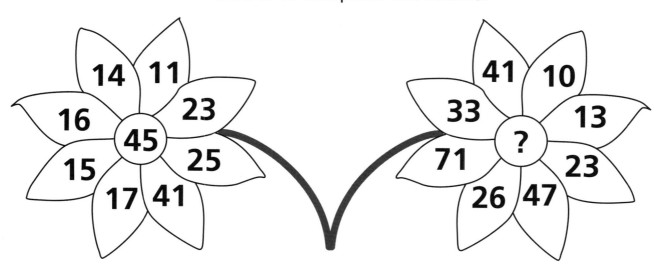

**18** What links the outer numbers to the inner one?

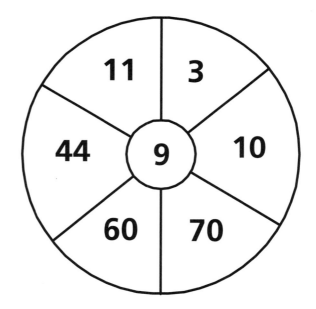

**19** Back in Victorian times, a shopkeeper had some weighing scales that he regularly used for measuring up to 40 pounds in weight of such items as sugar, flour and rice, in whole pounds only.

**What was the least number of weights that he needed in order to weigh accurately any amount up to 40 pounds?**

**20** A standard set of dominoes has been laid out, using numbers instead of dots for clarity. Using a sharp pencil and a keen brain, can you draw in the lines to show where each domino has been placed? You may find the check grid useful – crossing off each domino as you find it. One number has already been placed, to get you off to a good start.

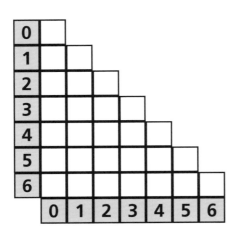

| 1 | 1 | 2 | 4 | 4 | 0 | 1 | 4 |
| 5 | 6 | 2 | 0 | 6 | 3 | 3 | 0 |
| 3 | 0 | 2 | 6 | 5 | 0 | 6 | 5 |
| 4 | 0 | 5 | 5 | 4 | 2 | 0 | 3 |
| 4 | 2 | 3 | 2 | 5 | 1 | 6 | 6 |
| 3 | 4 | 6 | 2 | 2 | 1 | 1 | 1 |
| 1 | 4 | 6 | 5 | 5 | 0 | 3 | 3 |

**1** Can you place the remaining dominoes in their correct positions, so that the total number of spots in each of the four rows and five columns equals the sum at the end of that row or column?

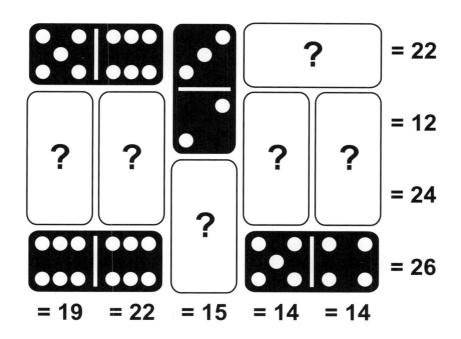

**2** Can you find the missing number?

# B42  D62  F82  H8-

**3** Which shape fits the hole – **A**, **B**, **C** or **D**? Any piece may be rotated but not flipped over.

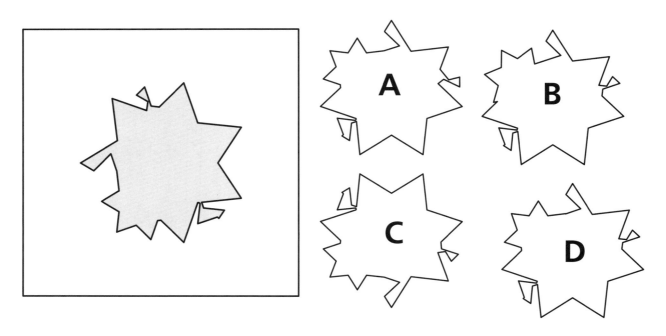

**4** Your watch is broken and your grandfather-clock stops one day, as you have forgotten to wind it.

There is a sudden power-cut to boot, and so you cannot listen to the radio or TV to find out the correct time.

Not wanting to wake anyone, there is no alternative – you will have to walk to the village and look at the clock in the general store's window – it is always reliable.

**How can you be sure to set your clock as accurately as possible when you get back?**

**5** Can you decipher the following message?

| | | | | | | | | | | |
|---|---|---|---|---|---|---|---|---|---|---|
| S | T | U | R | C | W | Y | B | T | M | S |
| T | L | H | A | E | I | R | R | Y | G | R |
| F | D | S | S | H | L | O | I | U | L | E |
| E | Y | A | H | T | L | F | G | B | A | P |
| L | U | C | G | R | H | K | F | O | N | A |
| E | P | E | O | E | E | C | L | T | Y | P |
| V | S | M | I | D | B | O | O | U | S | O |
| I | O | O | N | N | E | L | T | O | Y | W |

**6** You have four coconuts and know that only two of them are exactly the same weight.

Using a traditional two-pan balance, how many times at the most will you need to carry out a weighing operation in order to ascertain which two coconuts are identical in weight?

**7** What figure should replace the question mark in each of the following three instances?

# A. L2   VI3   XIII?

# B. XI3   LV4   LIV?

# C. XXII6   IX3   XVIII?

**8** An apartment block in New York has twenty-six floors – A through to Z. On each floor there are 72 flats.

If Mr Brown lives in flat 72A, Mr Green lives in flat 49F and Mr White lives in flat 65V, where might Mr Black live?

**9** Place the letters A, B, C, D, E, F, G, H, I and J into the empty spaces in the grid below, in such a way that each row and column, as well as each heavily outlined block of nine smaller squares contains a different letter of the alphabet.

| A |   |   | B |   | C |   |   | D |
|---|---|---|---|---|---|---|---|---|
|   | C |   |   | A |   |   | B |   |
|   |   | E |   |   | I | F |   |   |
| H |   |   | C |   | E |   |   | A |
|   | F |   |   |   |   |   | H |   |
| G |   |   | I |   | H |   |   | F |
|   |   | B | G |   |   | I |   |   |
|   | A | I |   | D |   |   | E |   |
| C |   |   | E |   | F |   |   | B |

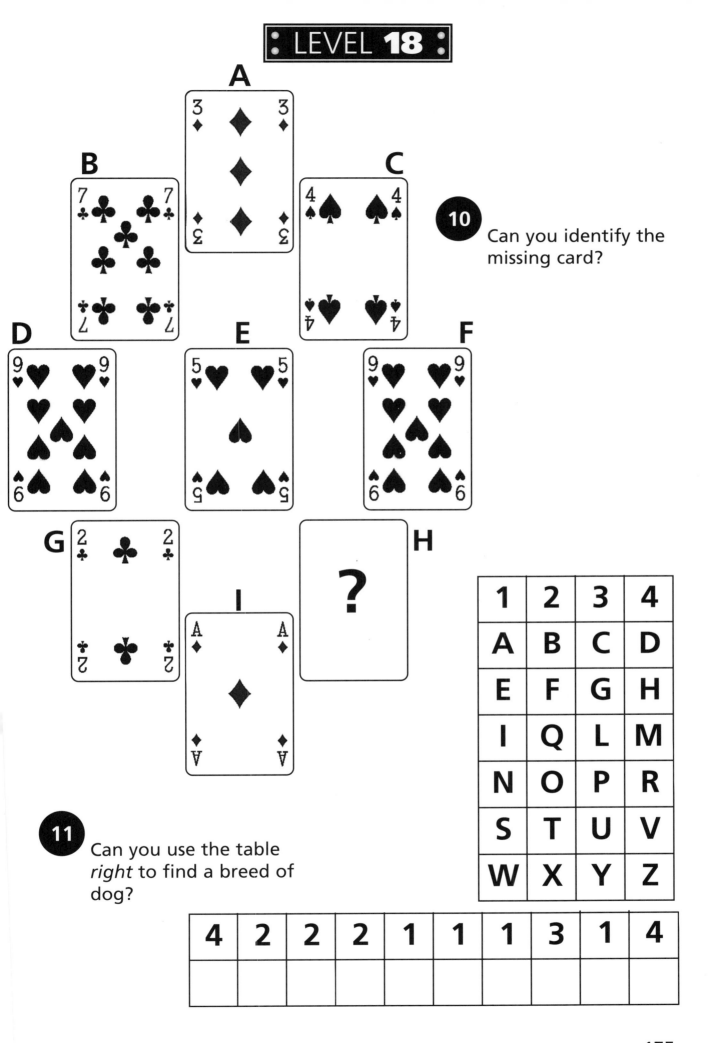

**A**

**B**

**C**

**10** Can you identify the missing card?

**D**

**E**

**F**

**G**

**I**

**H** ?

| 1 | 2 | 3 | 4 |
|---|---|---|---|
| A | B | C | D |
| E | F | G | H |
| I | Q | L | M |
| N | O | P | R |
| S | T | U | V |
| W | X | Y | Z |

**11** Can you use the table *right* to find a breed of dog?

| 4 | 2 | 2 | 2 | 1 | 1 | 1 | 3 | 1 | 4 |
|---|---|---|---|---|---|---|---|---|---|
| | | | | | | | | | |

**12** Can you rearrange these boxes to form three nine-letter words?

| ORK | FRA | ATE |
|-----|-----|-----|
| OUR | FAV | FUL |
| MIN | MEW | ITE |

**13** Which group of lines – **A**, **B**, **C**, **D** or **E** – should replace the question mark?

?

A       B       C

D       E

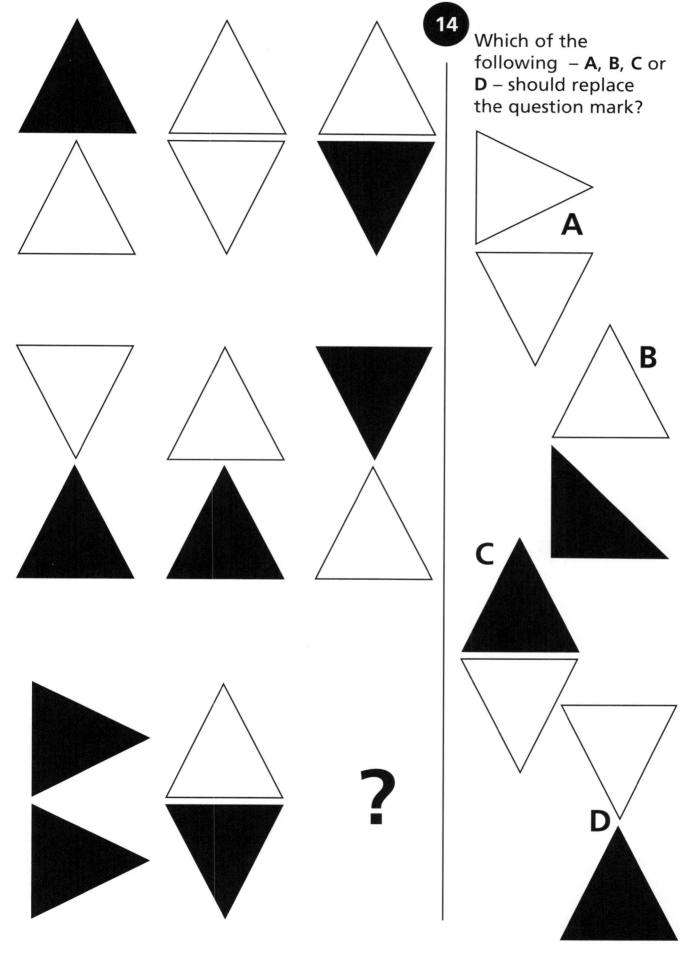

**14** Which of the following – **A**, **B**, **C** or **D** – should replace the question mark?

**15** What is the next number in this series?

**16** Can you fill in the missing numbers? The same logic applies to each horizontal row.

**A**

| 23879 | 3024 | ? |

**B**

| 61748 | ? | 48 |

**C**

| 99283 | ? | 1536 |

**17** The letters in the grid below are arranged in a logical pattern. Which tile completes the grid – **1**, **2**, **3** or **4**?

| A | C | D | D | E | C |
|---|---|---|---|---|---|
| B | E | C | F | B | D |
| F | B |   |   | E | F |
| A | B | F | F | E | A |
| C | E | A | D | B | E |
| D | B | C | C | D | F |

**1**

| A | A |
|---|---|

**2**

| A | D |
|---|---|

**3**

| D | B |
|---|---|

**4**

| E | A |
|---|---|

| 26 | 11 | 12 | 13 | 14 |
|----|----|----|----|----|
| 25 | 10 | 3  | 4  | 15 |
| 24 | 9  | 2  | ?  | 16 |
| 23 | 8  | 7  | 6  | 17 |
| 22 | 21 | 20 | 19 | 18 |

**18** What number should replace the question mark?

**1** What number completes the grid?

| 4 | 5 | 6 | 5 |
|---|---|---|---|
| 4 | 4 | 4 | 6 |
| 1 | 3 | 5 | 7 |
| 15 | 17 | 19 | ? |

**2** Which is the odd one out? Each is an anagram.

## AOHTTR
## CHOSAMT
## BAUILF
## ALAPTEL
## RGYIESN

**3** An absent-minded man is browsing in an antique shop and spots a 19th-century print that rather takes his fancy. It is dated with a year.

However, what he does not realise is that he is looking at the print upside-down.

This leads him to believe the print is 210 years older than it actually is.

**Can you work out what the date on the print must be?**

**4** Which letter is two places to the right of the letter which is four places above the letter two places to the right of the letter which is at the bottom of the column one place to the left of the column headed by N?

| A | N | F | O | I |
|---|---|---|---|---|
| M | B | S | V | P |
| Q | R | C | H | J |
| L | G | W | D | Y |
| T | X | U | K | E |

**5**   Can you place the discs into the correct spaces on the diagram so that the sums of all the outside edges to the hexagon are equal, and the sums of all the dissecting lines are also equal?

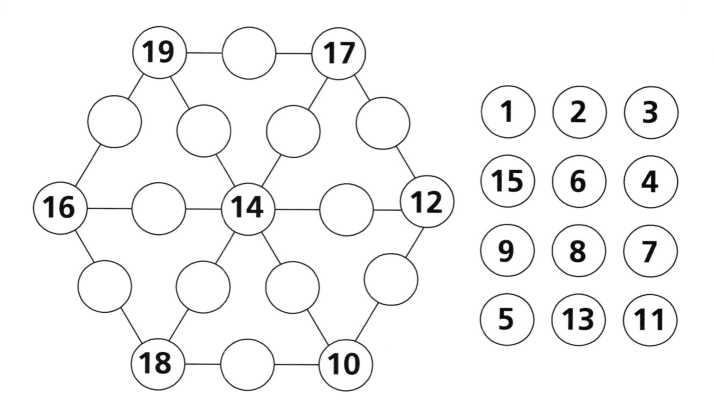

**6**   Which of the following three combinations of weights should you have if you would like to be able to weigh all measures up to and including 13 pounds in weight, in whole pounds, on a set of balancing scales?

**A. 6 pounds,   5 pounds,   2 pounds**
**B. 9 pounds,   3 pounds,   1 pound**
**C. 1 pound,    8 pounds,   4 pounds**

**7** What number consisting of two identical digits logically replaces the question mark?

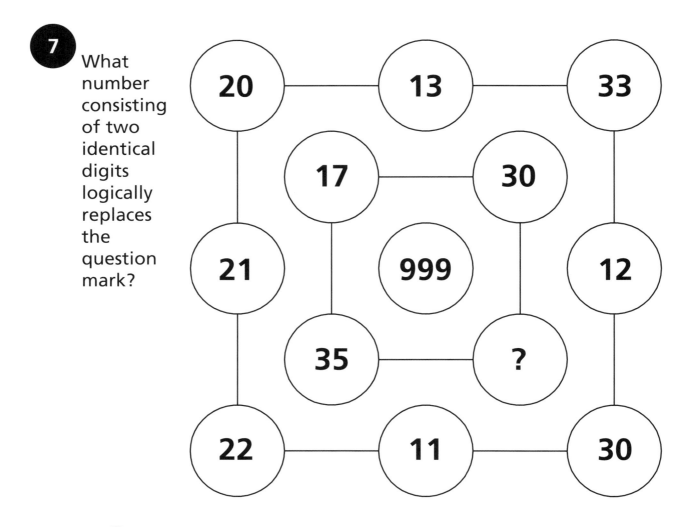

**8** What dial comes next in the series – **A**, **B**, **C** or **D**?

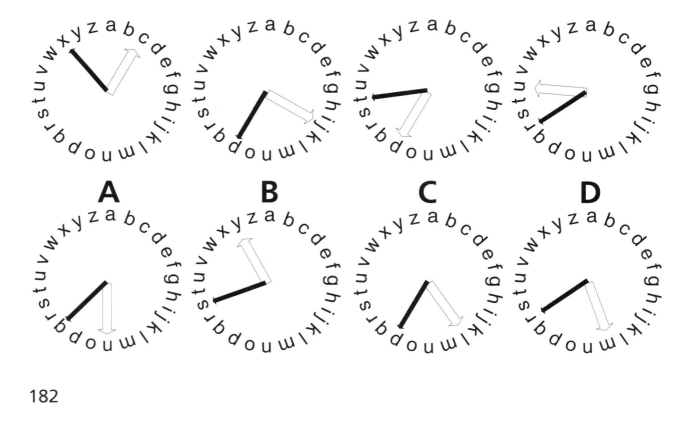

**A**  **B**  **C**  **D**

**9** Can you find a number which contains all digits from 1-9, except for 6, and which, when multiplied by 6, gives a number in which every single number from 1-9 appears? Each number should, in each instance, appear once only.

**10**

# ABLE  EFFORT  EXHAUST  TUNDRA

Which of the words given below could join the above, and why?

1. **MANDIBLE**
2. **EXHILERATE**
3. **ROUND**
4. **GREENERY**
5. **VALLEY**

6. **SPRITE**
7. **BECAUSE**
8. **VANDAL**
9. **STARRY**
10. **NORTHERN**

11. **RETINA**
12. **FRAUGHT**
13. **MONKEY**
14. **GIRAFFE**
15. **PORTENT**

**11** Imagine that you have 10 counters, each printed with a different number from 20-29. You then invite five friends – Janice, Irene, Mandy, Clive and Daryl – to pick 2 each.

Janice notices that the sum of the numbers on her two counters is 47, and that Irene's total comes to 51, Mandy's to 44, Clive's to 57, and Daryl's to 46.

**Who has which counters?**

**12** One of the bottom numbers is linked to one of the top letters. By starting with the numbered boxes, can you work out which two are linked? By the way, every second arrow you land on is showing the exact *opposite* of the way you should go.

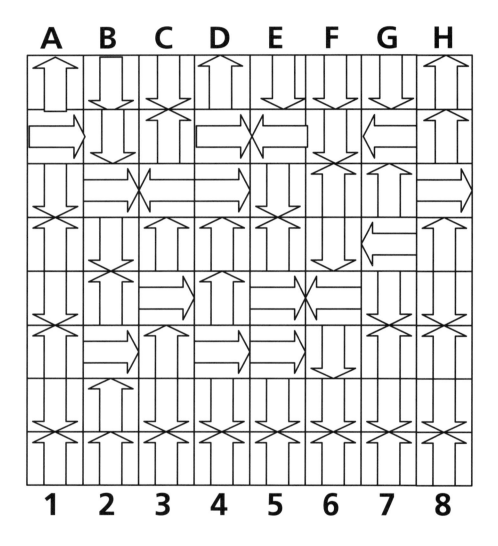

**13** What number comes next in the series?

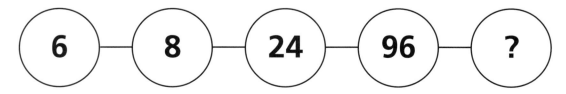

6 — 8 — 24 — 96 — ?

**14**

The accompanying diagram is a plan of a temple for that little-known Aztec prince, Lostalota. Doorways are represented by double arrows which link the outer rooms and the inner chambers.

By choosing the correct outer room as a starting point, it is possible to visit every room and inner chamber at least once, and to use every door once only.

Once you have chosen the correct starting point, there are numerous routes which will satisfy the above conditions but, whichever route you take, you will always end up in the same chamber. In which outer room must you always start, and in which inner chamber will you finish?

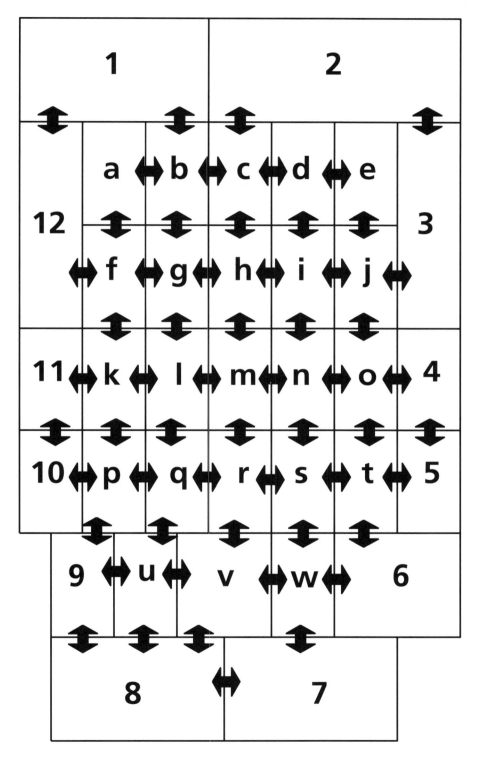

# LEVEL 19

**15** Can you arrange the following blocks containing the numbers 0–6, rotating them all to a vertical position so that they form a square, 6 blocks by 6 blocks, with no numbers repeated in any vertical or horizontal row.

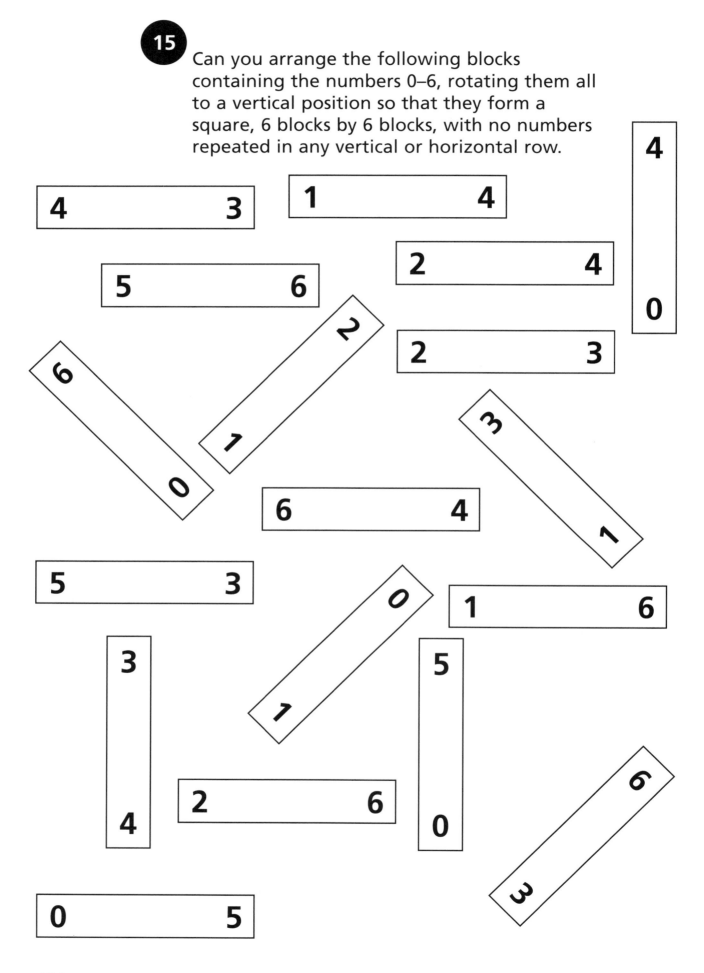

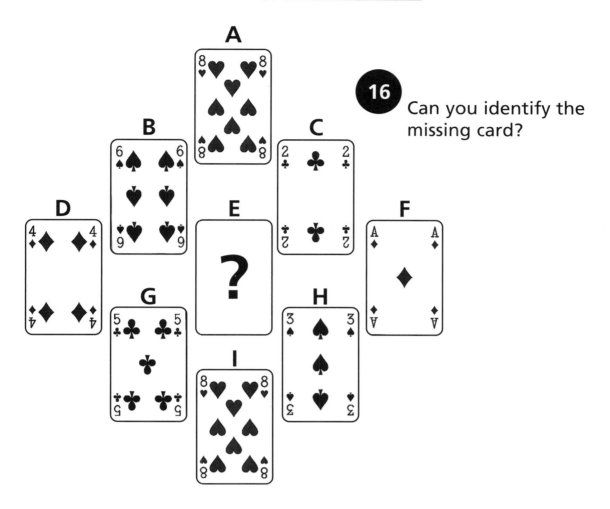

**16** Can you identify the missing card?

**17** Which letter do these pieces form when rearranged?

**1**

The security video camera has photographed 20 people on the escalator – 10 going up and 10 descending. In the diagram shown, each person is indicated by X. On either side of the escalator is a woman with her child immediately in front of her, and also a married couple, the wife being immediately in front in each case.

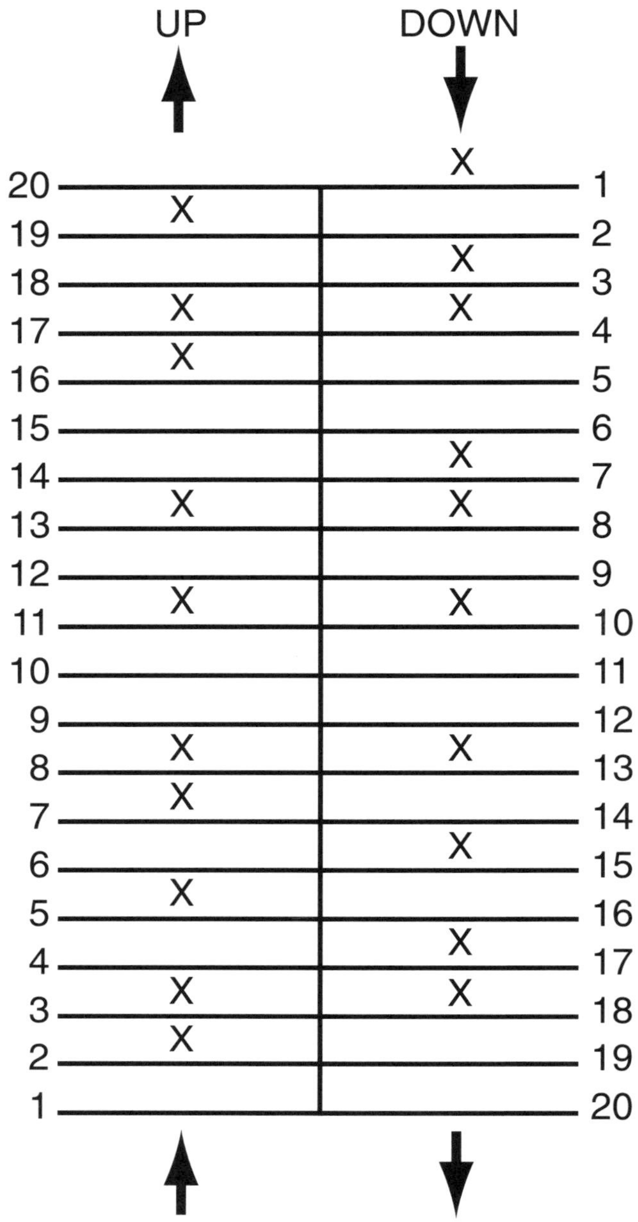

|  | UP ↑ | DOWN ↓ |  |
|---|---|---|---|
| 20 |  | X | 1 |
| 19 | X |  | 2 |
| 18 |  | X | 3 |
| 17 | X | X | 4 |
| 16 | X |  | 5 |
| 15 |  |  | 6 |
| 14 |  | X | 7 |
| 13 | X | X | 8 |
| 12 |  |  | 9 |
| 11 | X | X | 10 |
| 10 |  |  | 11 |
| 9 |  |  | 12 |
| 8 | X | X | 13 |
| 7 | X |  | 14 |
| 6 |  | X | 15 |
| 5 | X |  | 16 |
| 4 |  | X | 17 |
| 3 | X | X | 18 |
| 2 | X |  | 19 |
| 1 |  |  | 20 |
|  | ↑ | ↓ |  |

## UP

Mrs Jay is nearer the top than Mr Knight, who is five steps ahead of young Bobby Sims. Mr Fraser is ahead of Mrs Cox, who is with her husband. Ms Benson is at 16, and Mr Small is higher than Mrs Jay.

## DOWN

Miss Oliver is two steps ahead of Mrs Rowe, who is with her husband, and Mr Chalfont is three steps behind little Sally Vernon. There is one person between Miss Oliver and Mr Chalfont. Mr Lee is two steps behind Mr Donaldson.

Ms Wells is directly opposite Bobby and Mr Philips is directly opposite Mrs Jay. Miss Allen is opposite Miss Oliver.

Where is everybody?

|   |   |   |   |
|---|---|---|---|
| 1 | 5 | 4 | 5 |
| 3 | 7 | 8 | 0 |
| 2 | 6 | 3 | 4 |
| 7 | ? | 5 | 9 |

**2** What number completes the grid?

**3** Can you rearrange these boxes to form three nine-letter words?

| ADE | OUP | ARY |
|-----|-----|-----|
| DEC | MOT | SEC |
| OND | ORC | AGE |

**4** Can you punctuate the following so that it will be obvious what the meaning is?

# THAT THAT IS IS THAT THAT IS NOT IS NOT THAT THAT IS IS NOT THAT THAT IS NOT THAT THAT IS NOT IS NOT THAT THAT IS IS NOT THAT IT IT IS

**5** Imagine that you have three blue counters (B), three red counters (R) and three green counters (G), set out in the row of 11 boxes, as below. Thus there are two empty boxes at one side.

| B | R | G | B | R | G | B | R | G | | |
|---|---|---|---|---|---|---|---|---|---|---|

Your aim is to move the counters to form the pattern below.

| G | G | G | B | B | B | R | R | R | | |
|---|---|---|---|---|---|---|---|---|---|---|

However, there are certain rules. You can only move 2 adjacent counters each time, and the counters you move must remain together in the line-up. What is more, you cannot reverse their order. However, it is obviously fine to leave a gap between the letters at any time.

**Can you succeed in only 5 moves?**

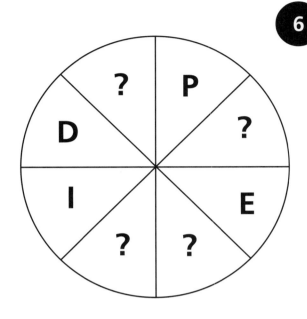

**6** If you insert the correct letters in the two circles shown, you will have two words with approximately the same meaning. One of the words reads in a clockwise direction, the other in an anticlockwise direction.

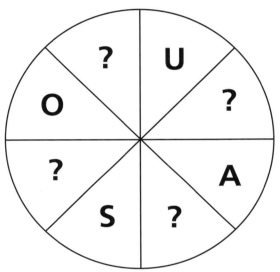

**7** Can you work out which of the following words would look the same in a mirror, if it were held perpendicular to this page? (Don't be tempted to cheat by using a mirror to start with; but, of course, check your answer afterwards.)

## BED  CAD  HOCK  EXILE  END
## HEX  DECK  STICK  COD  RED

**8** One of the bottom numbers is linked to one of the top letters. By starting with the numbered boxes, can you work out which two are linked? By the way, every second arrow you land on is showing the exact *opposite* of the way you should go.

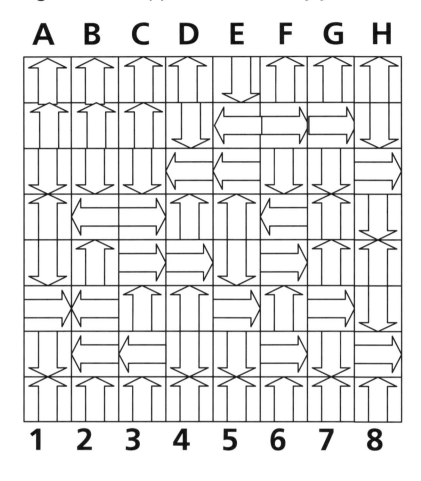

**9** What do each of the following words have in common?

# DEW   CHINZ   MOOT   GLOW
# ABBOT   IVY   FIST
# LOOPY   HILL

**10** What is the relationship between the central block (18) and the surrounding eight?

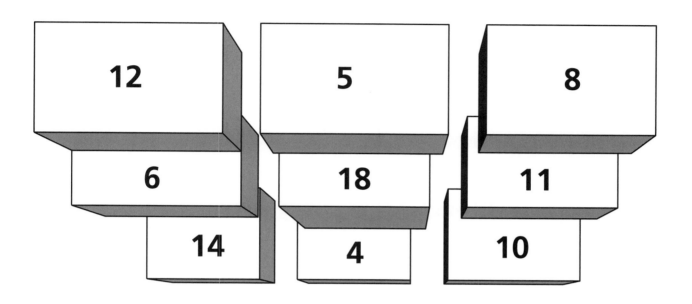

**11** In the BOOKULIKE Bookshop, the assistants are preparing for a signing session by the internationally renowned economist Emma Chizzit, to launch her new title *Last of the Big Spenders*.

Copies are piled up flat on a table, in four equal stacks. From one side, only 9 spines in each stack are visible because they are piled up alternately: in other words, any book lying on top of another will have its spine facing in exactly the opposite direction to that of the book below it.

**What is the least possible number of copies on the table?**

**12**  Can you solve the following encoded message?
Not for nothing is it the very last puzzle in this
compendium of brain-teasers!

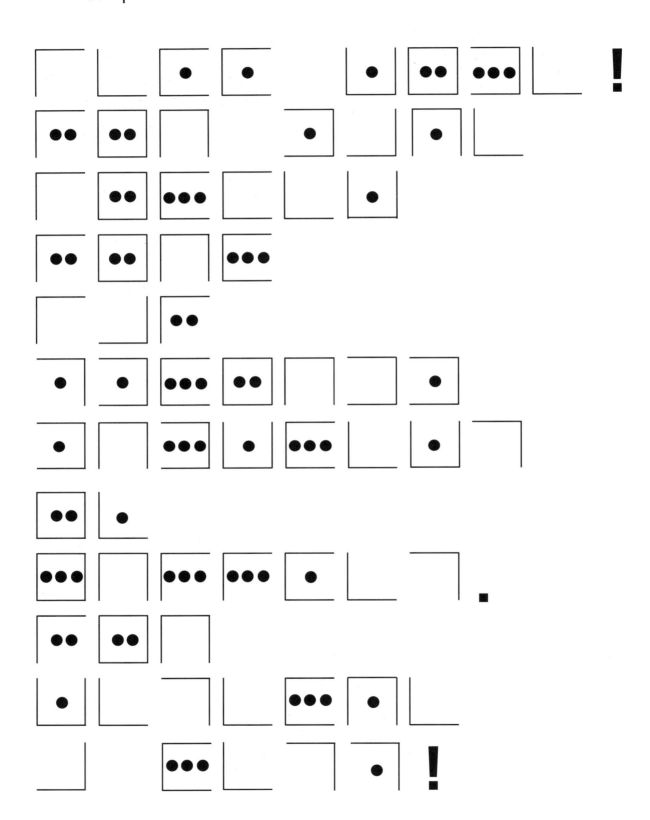

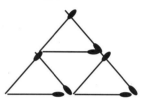

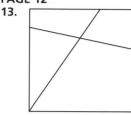

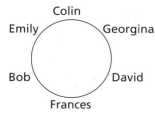

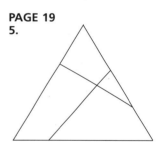

## LEVEL 1

**PAGE 7**
1. A. MAX
   B. GAVIN
   C. ERIC
   D. SID
   E. JOHN
   F. PAUL

2. 48. (The numbers increase by 15 on each balloon in ascending order.)

3.

| 11 | 4 | 9 |
|----|----|----|
| 6 | 8 | 10 |
| 7 | 12 | 5 |

**PAGE 8**
4. He simply unplaited the rope's strands and tied these together, ending up with a thinner, longer rope.

**PAGE 9**
5. 15. (The digits in the windows add up to the number on the door.)

6. 9. (The numbers progress from 1 and alternate.)

7. He is a joiner.

**PAGE 10**
8. Schumann

9. 15. (The number of sides of the two shapes are multiplied in each instance.)

10. P. (The letters run in alphabetical order in a counter-clockwise spiral.)

**PAGE 11**
11. Here is one possible solution:

Colin
Emily          Georgina
Bob              David
Frances

12. B, A, E, C, F, D or D, F, C, E, A, B (based on the number of straight lines making up each head.)

**PAGE 12**
13.

14. 10 per day. (Start from the time when she is only smoking 3 per day. The previous week, she would have been smoking 6 per day, as she cut down by 50 per cent. The week prior to that, she would have been smoking 8 per day, as she cut down by 25 per cent; and the week before, 10 per day, as she cut down by 20 per cent.)

15. 1C

16. Golf, tennis

**PAGE 13**
17. 20. (Each block is the sum of the two blocks directly below it.)

18. S, for SEVEN. (They are the initial letters of the first 7 numbers.)

19. 6 of Spades. (The suits progress and the values rise by one each time.)

**PAGE 14**
20. 7 x 4 + 2 = 30.

21. 18. (The numbers on the hands and feet add up to the numbers on the heads.)

22. Anna, scarf/ Mary, perfume/ Sarah, chocolates

**PAGE 15**
23. 18. (The numbers increase by 4 and clockwise.)

24. E.

25. BOMBASTIC, ABSORBENT, ESTABLISH

**PAGE 16**
26. 1. (No letter appears more than once in any horizontal, vertical or diagonal line.)

27. A.

## LEVEL 2

**PAGE 17**
1. ▢ = 5, △ = 4, ○ = 2, A

2. 21. (The numbers increase by 3 each time in an anticlockwise direction, starting at 3.)

**PAGE 18**
3. A. (The number of sides on each shape within the boxes increases by one on each higher level.)

4. There are 4 small equilateral triangles and one large one in this diagram.

**PAGE 19**
5.

6. 10, 14, 6, 24

7. He was her son.

**PAGE 20**
8. 24. (The head is the product of the hands and feet: 1 x 2 x 3 x 4.)

9. I. (Look at the cross in the central right-hand box.)

**PAGE 21**
10. XLVIII. (The Roman numerals double each time as the balloons get higher, starting with VI or 6.)

11. 2B

12. C

13. 3. (All the linked circles add up to 15.)

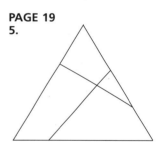

SOLUTIONS – SOLUTIONS – SOLUTIONS – SOLUTIONS – SOLUTIONS

195

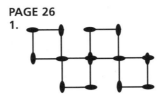

**PAGE 22**
14. MEDUSA

15. 11. (The numbers in each triangle add up to 25.)

16. 3 girls and 4 boys.

**PAGE 23**
17. Jack of Spades. (The suits progress and the values rise by two each time.)

18. 6 ÷ 2 x 5 = 15

19. S, for SUNDAY. (They are the initial letters of the days of the week, beginning with Monday.)

**PAGE 24**
20. Each drove the other's car. (The will had specified that the estate should go to the brother whose car crossed the finishing line in second place. Swapping cars, the brothers drove flat out, according to the rules. It was the aim of each to win and cross the finishing line first, however, so that his own car came second and therefore provided him with the additional inheritance.)

**PAGE 25**
21. 2. (The figures in the central column are the sums of the numbers on their right and left.)

22. HALLMARKS, IMPARTIAL, AUXILIARY

23. None. (He was on the bottom rung when he fell!)

**PAGE 26**
1.

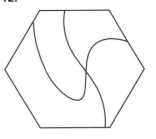

2. J & T. (Each letter on the top line progresses by three, and on the bottom line goes back by two.)

3. 5 people

**PAGE 27**
4.

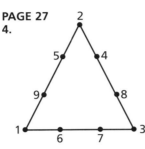

5. Ace, Queen, 2, 8, 3, Jack, 4, 9, 5, King, 6, 10 and 7, with the Ace starting at the top of the pack.

**PAGE 28**
6. A3

7. 10. (The horizontal rows all add up to 21.)

8. The secret of success with this puzzle is to start each time with the coin that is two coins before the coin you started counting with previously. (You will find another similar puzzle elsewhere in this book, involving cards.)

**PAGE 29**
9. 10. (The sum of the hands less the sum of the feet equals the number on the head.)

10. 16. (The first six squared numbers are shown in a clockwise direction – that is, 1 x 1 = 1, 2 x 2 = 4, 3 x 3 = 9, 4 x 4 = 16, 5 x 5 = 25, 6 x 6 = 36.)

11. 8. (In each triangle, the bottom right number is the product of the other two.)

**PAGE 30**
12.

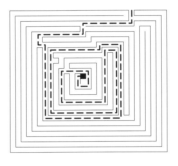

13. E. (Look at the bottom righthand circle.)

**PAGE 31**
14.

15. D

16. 132. (Take away 45 each time.)

**PAGE 32**
17. RICHARD BURTON

18. Annie $15,000 and Steve $11,000/ Barbara $10,000 and Chris $10,000/ Sue $14,000 and Bill $8,000

**PAGE 33**
19. B. (The number of sides on each shape within the boxes increases by two on each higher level.)

20. NAVIGATOR, GALLANTRY, BEAUTIFUL

**PAGE 34**
21. A

22. Queen of Spades. (The suits progress and the value rises by two each time.)

23. J. (They are the initial letters of the first six months of the year.)

**PAGE 35**
24. Will would provide a list of words, from each of which Dill knew he had to take the third letter until they made a whole word.

25. 3333. (The 20 digits in any vertical column, horizontal row or diagonal line add up to 110.)

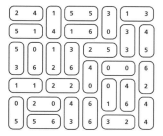

## PAGE 36
1.

## PAGE 37
2. 9 of Diamonds. (Each row, vertical column and diagonal line adds up to 15. Only 3 suits are used, and none appears more than once in any line.)

3. 21. (The head equals twice the sum of the hands less the sum of the feet.)

## PAGE 38
4. L. (The numerical value of each letter is the sum of the numerical values of the two letters directly below it: B = 2, D = 4, H = 8, F = 6, R = 18.)

5. Jump 5 over 8, then 9, then 3 and then 1. Jump 7 over 4. Jump 6 over 2 and then 7. Jump 5 over 6.

6. Each shelf is obviously 50cm (20in) + 50cm (20in) long = 1m (40in) long. As there were two shelves of this length, the original plank could have been 2m (80in) in length. But the question asks how *short* the plank could have been. Fred might, for example, have sawn the plank in half along its length to make narrower shelves, in which case the plank might only have been 1m (40in) long.

## PAGE 39
7. $\triangle$ = 9, $\square$ = 5, $\bigcirc$ = 2, C

8. A

9. 60. (The series descends by 16, 8, 4 and then 2.)

## PAGE 40
10. B

11. 125. (The first cubed numbers are shown in a counter-clockwise direction - that is,
1 x 1 x 1 = 1,
2 x 2 x 2 = 8,
3 x 3 x 3 = 27.
4 x 4 x 4 = 64,
5 x 5 x 5 = 125,
6 x 6 x 6 = 216.)

12. SPAIN / AUSTRIA

## PAGE 41
13. 27 594 16038.
(27 x 594 = 16038.
594 = 27 x 22 and is therefore a multiple of 27. Each digit from 0 – 9 is used once only.)

14.

## PAGE 42
15. F. (Look at the bottom point of the central star.)

16. Alice is 38 and her husband is 42.

## PAGE 43
17. Slow. (All the others are verbs, whereas 'slow' requires 'up' or 'down' to become a verb.)

18. 56. (The numbers double on each balloon in ascending order.)

19. N.
(1. China,
2. Poland,
3. Nigeria,
4. Lapland,
5. Norway,
6. Yemen.)

## PAGE 44
20. 34 + 41 ÷ 5 – 14 = 1

21. NARRATIVE, PARASITES, WATERMARK

22. C2

## PAGE 45
23. 7. (The two lower numbers in each triangle add up to the top one.)

24. 60. (Each block is the sum of the two blocks below it, plus the sum of the two blocks beneath them, etc.)

25. ALAIN PROST

## PAGE 46
1. How could anyone know about Philip's dream if he died before he woke and was able to tell anyone about it?

2. E. (In all the others, the first three digits add up to the last.)

## PAGE 47
3. Since they drank equal quantities, each man consumed one-third of a gallon or $2^2/_3$ pints. Tom supplied 5 pints and drank $2^2/_3$ pints, so he contributed $2^1/_3$ pints. Jack supplied 3 pints and drank $2^2/_3$ pints, so he contributed $^1/_3$ pint. As this was only $^1/_7$ of the amount that Tom contributed, it is fair to say that Tom should receive $7 and Jack $1.

4. A. (Each shape appears once only in each row or column, and in one of the three positions.)

## PAGE 48
5. 5. GIRAFFE.
(The others are
1. SWALLOW,
2. ROBIN,
3. NIGHTINGALE,
4. OSTRICH.)

6. PARTHENON

7. FIREMAN / SOLDIER

## PAGE 49
8. 81

9. A = ANDREW;
B = FRANK;
C = CHARLIE;
D = JAMES:
E = EDWARD.

## PAGE 50
10. There are 34 complete single squares; 22 two by two; 12 three by three; and 5 four by four, giving a total of 73.

**11.** 74. (First of all, he made 50 new cigarettes. Then, after he had smoked them, from the 50 butts, he could make 16 further cigraettes, saving the two extra butts. From the 16 new cigarettes, which left 16 butts, he could make 5 more new cigarettes, and had one butt over. He then added this one to the two previously saved, and made an extra cigarette. Now he had 6 new cigarettes and, after smoking them, could make 2 new cigarettes from the butts. However, the remaining 2 butts from these were insufficient for another cigarette – though, being parsimonious by nature, he probably kept them for possible future use!)

**PAGE 51**
**12.** 2

**PAGE 52**
**13.** C

**14.** 18. (The horizontal rows, vertical columns and diagonal lines all add up to 30.)

**PAGE 53**
**15.** D

**16.** BALACLAVA, MAHARAJAH, BARBARIAN

**17.**

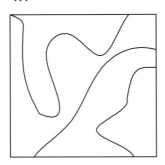

**PAGE 54**
**18.** The diagram that follows shows the pattern you can form from 24 matches to give 8 small triangles, 4 bigger ones, 4 bigger ones still and 4 even larger ones – 20 in all. There are also 4 small squares, one larger one and one larger one still.

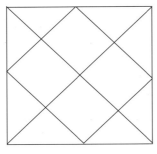

**19.** 8. (The last figure in each horizontal row is the sum of the first three.)

**20.** £1,800.

**PAGE 55**
**1.** This is how you should proceed:
Move a white block from space 3 to 4.
Jump a black from 5 to 3.
Move a black from 6 to 5.
Jump a white from 4 to 6.
Jump a white from 2 to 4.
Move a white from 1 to 2.
Jump a black from 3 to 1.
Jump a black from 5 to 3.
Jump a black from 7 to 5.
Move a white from 6 to 7.
Jump a white from 4 to 6.
Jump a white from 2 to 4.
Move a black from 3 to 2.
Jump a black from 5 to 3.
Move a white from 4 to 5.
That's it!

**2.** 27, 28, 29

**3.** AESTHETIC, TREACHERY, CELESTIAL

**PAGE 56**
**4.** C. (The outer and inner shapes can be either square, round or triangular. The inner shapes are either black or white. None of the above repeats in any horizontal row or vertical column.)

**5.** 8. (The last number in each vertical column is the sum of the first three.)

**6.** 1 & A

**PAGE 57**
**7.** A. She put 6 to the left of 5 and 4 to the left of 1.
B. She placed 6 on top of 3.

**8.** A

**9.** 41. (The numbers progress from 1 in an anticlockwise direction, each being 1 less than 3 times the last.)

**10.** 23. (The sequence runs + 5 / –3 alternately.)

**PAGE 58**
**11.**

**12.** The size and number of each possible rectangle is given *below*.

2 x 1 = 55; 3 x 1 = 42;
4 x 1 = 30; 5 x 1 = 18;
6 x 1 = 10; 7 x 1 = 2;
3 x 2 = 33; 4 x 2 = 23;
5 x 2 = 13; 6 x 2 = 7;
7 x 2 = 1; 4 x 3 = 16;
5 x 3 = 8; 6 x 3 = 4;
5 x 4 = 4; 6 x 4 = 2

This gives a total of 268.

**13.** 45. (Add ascending pairs of balloons to arrive at the next balloon in each case.)

**PAGE 59**
**14.** C. (The internal shapes rotate clockwise, and the top left shape is always black.)

**15.** C. (Look in a mirror!)

**PAGE 60**
**16.** They borrowed one cat from another breeder, so that there were 18 in all once more. Then one son took his half share – that is, 9. The second son took his third share – 6; and the third son took his ninth share – just 2. This left the borrowed cat which they gave back to its rightful owner. Of course, if the deceased cat had lived, there always would have been one cat left over or they would have had to resort to sharing for, in spite of her wealth, their mother was no mathematician and did not realise that one-half plus one-third plus one-ninth comes to less than a whole number!

**17.** 1.E. 2.W. 3.U. 4.E.

**PAGE 61**
**18.** WINSTON CHURCHILL

**19.** D. (The white pointer moves forwards two letters each time, while the black pointer moves forwards three letters each time.)

**PAGE 62**
**20.** 49. (The numbers on the left are the squares of their opposite numbers.)

**21.** 13. (The central number in each triangle is the sum of the other three.)

**22.** The number of spots on opposite sides of a die totals 7, thus the two hidden vertical faces of the top die have 3 and 5 spots, the two hidden vertical faces of the central die have 4 and 5 spots and the two hidden vertical faces of the bottom die have 1 and 2 spots: this adds up to 20 (3+5+4+5+1+2).

**PAGE 63**
**23.** 216. (The smaller number in the verticsally connected shapes is the cube root of the larger one.)

**24.** You can start where you like, but you need to begin each subsequent series of moves so that the card you will be turning over is the one that you touched in the previous sequence. Thus, if you touched the card that is top left and proceeded to the right, turning over the card at top right, the next card that you touch should be the card second from the top right, so that you next turn over the card at the bottom right.

**PAGE 64**
**25.** Cake, $9/ biscuits, $1.50. (Think of the biscuits as costing one unit and the cake, 6 units – that is, six times as much. Seven units altogether come to $10.50. So one unit (the biscuits) must have cost $1.50.)

**26.** 48. (The top number divided by the bottom gives the central number, as does the lefthand number multiplied by the righthand number.)

**27.** D. (In all the others, an angular shape is on the outside.)

**PAGE 65**
**1.** $\triangle = 6$, $\square = 9$, $\bigcirc = 1$, B

**2.** N

**3.** William is $(34 \div 2) - 14 = 3$.
His mother is $14 + 3 + 9 = 26$.

**PAGE 66**
**4.** 64. (The numbers on the left are the cubes of those opposite.)

**5.** 3,500 infantry = 7,000 legs and 730 cavalry = 1,460 riders' legs and 2,920 horses' legs = 4,380 legs. 766 artillery = 1532 legs, Sir Henry provides a further 2 legs, and we should also count his tripod (3 legs) to give a total of 12,917 legs.

**PAGE 67**
**6.** D

**7.** The total length of the fish was the head (5cm/2in) and body (20cm/8in) and tail (15cm/6in) = 40cm (16in). (The head was 5cm (2in) long, we are told. The tail was 5cm (2in) long, plus half of the body part. The body part was 5cm (2in) + 5cm (2in) + half of the body part, so that the body must have measured 20cm (2in). The tail therefore measured 5cm (2in) + 10cm (4in).)

**PAGE 68**
**8.** Michael. (If Billy had done it, what both Michael and Douglas said would be true, but we know that only one of the boys told the truth. If Rupert did it, what Billy, Michael and Douglas said would be true, which again could not be the case. If Douglas did it, what Rupert and Michael said would be true, which once more cannot be so. By deduction, therefore, it was Michael who was guilty, and Douglas was the only boy telling the truth.)

**9.** N. (The other letters spell the word FOOTBALL.)

**PAGE 69**
**10.** B. (A shape appears once only in every horizontal row or vertical column.)

**11.**
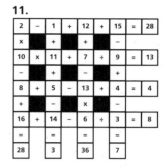

**PAGE 70**
**12.** 4. Tomato (a fruit). The others are anagrams for carrot, parsnip, swede, celery.

**13.** B. (The white pointer advances three letters each time and the black pointer moves forwards four letters each time.)

**PAGE 71**
**14.**
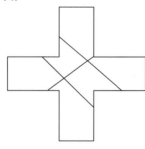

**15.** CIGARETTE, COLLEAGUE, SCAVENGER

**16.** 12. (The numbers in the central triangle are the products of the corresponding numbers in the two other triangles.)

**PAGE 72**
**17.** 19 scarves, 1 pair of tights and 80 beads.

**18.** SPAGHETTI / PANCAKE

## LEVEL 8

## LEVEL 9

**PAGE 73**
**19.** RAINBOW WARRIOR

**20.** Jim 36 and Laura 27/
Gavin 32 and Sarah 33/
Mervin 29 and
Eleanor 24/
Spike 30 and Rosie 30/
Grant 28 and Helen 25.

**PAGE 74**
**21.**

**22.** 55. (You need to
count the one big square,
and squares that are
4 x 4, 3 x 3, 2 x 2 and
1 x 1.)

**23.** First you should put
the string down on the
table. Then fold your
arms and hold the left
end of the string with
your right hand and the
right end with your left.
Now unfold your arms.
You should find that you
have made a knot in the
string.

**PAGE 75**
**1.** □ = 5, ○ = 12, △ = 7, A.

**2.** 10 hens

**PAGE 76**
**3.** 10. (The numbers
progress in the following
way, starting with
1: 1 + 2 = 3, 3 + 3 = 6,
6 + 4 = 10, 10 + 5 = 15,
15 + 6 = 21.)

**4.** 6 x 7 – 4 + 3 = 41
  x  x  x  x
  4 + 3 x 9 – 8 = 55
  +  +  ÷  +
  9 x 5 + 2 – 1 = 46
  ÷  –  –  ÷
  3 x 6 – 8 x 5 = 50
  =  =  =  =
  11 20 10  5

**PAGE 77**
**5.** 1897

**6.** 1. (N has one fewer
line than M, and I has
one fewer line than T.)

**PAGE 78**
**7.** B. (Silk is the only
animal-based fibre.)

**8.** B.

**9.** 31. (They are the
number of days in the
first few months of an
ordinary year.)

**PAGE 79**
**10.** 64
   11
(Each top number
decreases by 23, 21, 19
and 17, and is also a
squared number, starting
with 12 and ending with
8 squared, and each
bottom number
decreases by 1.)

**11.** I.

**12.** ELEPHANT / LEOPARD

**PAGE 80**
**13.** 312132

**14.** 64. (The number on
each balloon is the sum
of balloons below it.)

**15.** Carry an umbrella.

**16.** B. (In the others,
digits are in ascending
order.)

**PAGE 81**
**17.** OCCUPANTS,
ENCHANTED,
COCKTAILS.

**18.**

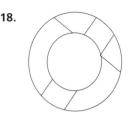

**19.** 54. (The central
number in each triangle
is half the product of the
other three.)

**20.** P. (The letters
advance in the series
1, 2, 4, 8, 16.)

**PAGE 82**
**21.** The secret lies in
making sure that you
make the end of your
second move (where you
leave a coin) the starting
point of the first,
continuing in this way.
So, if as the result of your
first move, you place a
coin on 4, having started
on 1, you should then
move from 6 to 1, leaving
a coin on 1.

**PAGE 83**
**22.** S. (Each first letter is
the initial letter of the
capital city of the
European country to
which it belongs. The
first letter of that country
is given after each
oblique. So the pairs are:
London/England;
Paris/France;
Vienna/Austria;
Madrid/Spain;
Oslo/Norway; and
Warsaw/Poland.)

**23.** 12. (The numbers in
the first tile add up to 5,
the second, 10, and so
on, in 5s.)

**24.** C. (The white pointer
moves backwards two
letters each time, and the
black pointer moves
forwards two letters.)

**PAGE 84**
**1.** 6. (The individual digits
in each triangle add up
to 21.)

**2.**

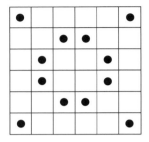

**PAGE 85**
**3.** The front line will
move tomorrow.
(Each letter represents
the one that is before of
after it in the alphabet,
alternately.)

**4.** The waitress knew that
he wanted cream
because he put down
one 50 cent piece and
five 10 cent pieces. If he
had not wanted cream,
he would have put down
one 50 cent piece and
just four 10 cent pieces.
(No tip was called for in
respect of a simple cup of
coffee at a bar.)

**5.** The outer numbers
increase by a factor of 2
each time, in a counter-
clockwise direction.

**PAGE 86**
**6.** 10

**7.** KILIMANJARO

**PAGE 87**
**8.** G

**9.** HELICOPTER/TRAM

**10.** B. (The white
pointer moves
backwards three
letters each time
and the black pointer
moves forwards five
letters each time.)

**PAGE 88**
**11.** WHITEBAIT,
HERBALIST,
BOATHOUSE

**12.**

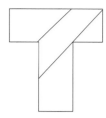

**13.** 8 and 4.

**14.** 16. (The numbers in the third triangle are the sum of the corresponding numbers in the first-two.)

**PAGE 89**
**15.** A. (Amber is fossilized tree resin, while the others are all mineral-based.)

**16.** 16. (The right hand less the left hand multiplied by the right foot less the left foot equals the figure in the head.)

**17.** Oliver and Gordon were indeed brothers, but neither was the other's brother!

**PAGE 90**
**18.** C. (No symbol appears more than once in any horizontal, vertical or diagonal row.)

**PAGE 91**
**19.** 51. (The sum of the numbers on progressive tiles doubles each time.)

**20.** 45 minutes only as the alarm, of course, went off at 11.00pm.

**21.** 227. (The number on each ascending balloon is three times the last, plus five.)

**PAGE 92**
**22.** C

**23.** 20 mm. (This is the distance between the two covers. The worm does not travel through pages in this instance as the first page of Volume `I is only 2 covers away from the last page of Volume II.)

**PAGE 93**
**24.** △ = 9, ○ = 2, ❏ = 15, C

**25.** Amy gets 15, Sally gets 16, Eddie gets 15, and Paul gets only 4. (The best way to start is to draw up a table, listing the sweets as they are distributed.)

| Amy | Sally | Eddie | Paul |
|---|---|---|---|
| 1 | 2 | 3 | |
| 4, 5 | 6 | 7 | |
| 8 | 9,10 | 12 | 11 |
| 13 | 14, 15 | 16 | |
| 17 | 18 | 19, 20 | 21 |
| 22 | 23 | 24, 25 | |
| 26 | 27 | 28 | |
| 29, 30 | 32 | 33 | 31 |
| 34, 35 | 36 | 37 | |
| 38 | 39, 40 | 42 | 41 |
| 43 | 44, 45 | 46 | |
| 47 | 48 | 49, 50 | |

**PAGE 94**
**1.**

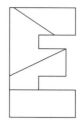

**2.** Falconers, Craftsmen, Lethargic

**3.** 57. (The digits of the lower numbers add up to the top number in each instance, with the first lower digit increasing by one each time.)

**PAGE 95**
**4.** D. (The white pointer moves forward five letters each time, while the black pointer moves back four letters each time.)

**5.** 4. CHOCOLATE. (The others are
1. RHUBARB
2. BANANA
3. NECTARINE
4. PINEAPPLE
5. GRAPEFRUIT.)

**PAGE 96**
**6.** 1. (The score is based on the number of Es in each name.)

**7.** The righthand numbers are the sum of their opposites plus the centre.

**8.** 42 euros.

**PAGE 97**
**9.** C. (The number of spaces in the third box of each row is equal to the sum of the spaces in the first two.)

**10.** 5 and F

**11.** 30. (The numbers in the last triangle are the products of the corresponding numbers in the first two triangles.)

**PAGE 98**
**12.** The lawyer was the only man, and the waiter heard his low voice when he shouted.

**13.**

| 17 | 16 | 10 | 29 | 23 |
|---|---|---|---|---|
| 24 | 18 | 12 | 11 | 30 |
| 31 | 25 | 19 | 13 | 7 |
| 8 | 27 | 26 | 20 | 14 |
| 15 | 9 | 28 | 22 | 21 |

**14.** If you add up the numerical values of each letter in the individual fruits, you arrive at a total which gives its price per kilo. One kilo of grapes therefore costs 7 + 18 + 1 + 16 + 5 + 19 = 66 cents, and so a half-kilo comes to 33 cents

**PAGE 99**
**15.** THE MERCHANT OF VENICE

**16.** B. (In the third shape in each row, the second is superimposed on the first.)

**PAGE 100**
**17.** G. (A can be paired with E, B with F, C with I, and D with H.)

## LEVEL 11

**PAGE 101**

**1.** 11 rows. (The difference between 160 and 580 is 420. You might therefore take a guess and see if there could be about 11 rows, counting the first and last, with 42 more plants in each successive row. It is a reasonable starting point and might turn out to be right. If it is too high or too low, you will at least know in which direction to try again. Now write out a table, as shown, to see if 11 rows will in fact give you 4,070 plants.

Row 1  160
Row 2  202
Row 3  244
Row 4  286
Row 5  328
Row 6  370
Row 7  412
Row 8  454
Row 9  496
Row 10 538
Row 11 580
Total: 4,070

So 11 rows is indeed right after all!)

**2.** B. 2487790844. (The first figure decreases by 1, the second increases by 2, and so on, alternately.)

**3.** One thousand

**PAGE 102**

**4.** The inner number is the sum of the outer numbers.

**5.** 11. (The sum of the numbers on each figure is 30.)

**6.** C.

**PAGE 103**

**7.** 4: The figures in the linked circles add up to the centre circle.

**8.** 40. (Starting with 5, use the following sequence:
5 + 1 = 6; 6 + 1 + 2 = 9;
9 + 1 + 2 + 3 = 15;
15 + 1 + 2 + 3 + 4 = 25;
25 + 1 + 2 + 3 + 4 + 5 = 40.)

**9.** MICHELANGELO

**PAGE 104**

**10.**

**11.** 9. (The sum of the first two numbers in each vertical column, minus the third, gives the fourth.)

**12.** TYMPANIST, STRIATION, PAINTWORK

**PAGE 105**

**13.** G. (A can be paired with I, B with H, C with E, and D with F.)

**14.** One bag of sand weighs 4kg (9lb). One bag of sugar weighs $^2/_3$kg (1$^1/_3$lb).

**PAGE 106**

**15.** D

**16.** 50. (The centre number is the sum of the numbers on the petals in each case.)

**PAGE 107**

**17.** C. (The shapes repeat every fourth place, and the hatching repeats every third place.)

**18.** 24. (The top numbers plus one-half of the bottom numbers add up to 30 in each case.)

**19.** A. (The white pointer advances two letters each time, while the black pointer advances eight letters each time.)

**PAGE 108**

**20.** 17. (The numbers in the middle triangle are the sums of the corresponding numbers in the two other triangles.)

**21.** 737. (Multiply the first number by 2, then add 4; multiply by 3 and add 5; multiply by 4 and add 6, etc.)

**22.** ❑ = 6, ◯ = 4, △ = 5, B

**PAGE 109**

**23.** D4

**24.** 11. (Twice the bottom left number plus the bottom right number equals the top number.)

**25.** BARBARY

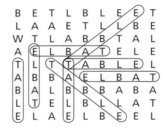

**PAGE 110**

**26.** 8.

## LEVEL 12

**PAGE 111**

**1.** 36. (In each flower, the centre number is the product of any two opposite petals.)

**2.** HELLO! (Hold the book horizontally to your eyes and all will become clear.)

**PAGE 112**

**3.** 417:21, 928:56, 846:24. (The second digit is subtracted from the first in each instance and then multiplied by the third to give the figure after the colon.)

**4.** A triangle. (Triangles are inserted if the numbers produce a total that is odd; squares, if the total is even.)

**5.** 0,4,6; 0,5,5; 1,3,6; 1,4,5; 2,2,6; 2,3,5; 2,4,4; 3,3,4 – thus there are 8 ways.

**PAGE 113**

**6.** △ = 9, ◯ = 17, ❑ = 4, B

**7.** 13.5 (Halve each number and add 4 to give the next number. There is no reason to suppose the answer must be a whole number.)

**8.** A1

**PAGE 114**

**9.** B. (The white pointer moves forwards 1,2,3,4 etc. letters each time, while the black pointer moves backwards 2,4,6,8 etc. letters each time.)

**10.** 1 Policeman
2 Electrician
3 Hairdresser
4 Banker
5 Designer
6 Journalist
7 Undertaker
8 Salesman
9 Lifeguard
10 Accountant

**PAGE 115**

**11.** If you add up the numerical values for each letter in the surnames of the residents, you arrive at the following: Jim PETERS 83 (16 + 5 + 20 + 5 + 18 + 19), Paul JONES 63, Harry SMITH 69, Jessica CLARK 45. If you then add up the individual digits of these totals you get 11, 9, 15 and 9 respectively. As these numbers correspond to the individual house numbers, Jessica Clark, according to this logic, is living with Paul Jones.

**12.** 4 darts in ring 23 = 92/ 1 dart in ring 18 = 18/ 1 dart in ring 15 = 15. Or 4 darts in ring 21, 1 in 23, and 1 in 18.

**13.** D. (All of the others are squared numbers – that is:
A. 35 x 35 = 1225;
B. 44 x 44 = 1936;
C. 43 x 43 = 1849;
E. 45 x 45 = 2025.)

**PAGE 116**
**14.**

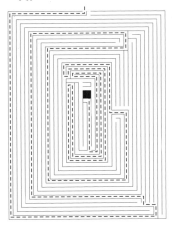

**PAGE 117**
**15.** TRANSFORM, TEMPORARY, MARQUETRY

**16.** 10. (Each row of three circles going through the central one adds up to 22.)

**PAGE 118**
**17.** 17. (The numbers on the third figure are the sums of the corresponding numbers on the first and second figures.)

**18.** 10. (The top numbers are half the bottom numbers plus 1.)

**19.** B. (The number of dots goes up by one each time.)

**PAGE 119**
**20.** The inner number is the product of all the outer numbers.

**21.** 6. (The top number in each triangle is twice the sum of the bottom two.)

**22.** B.

**PAGE 120**
**23.** 1280 x 39 - 5 x 8 = 399,320

**24.** ORINOCO

**25.** 29. (After giving the letters a numerical value according to their place in the alphabet, the figure at the end of each row is the sum of these numbers.)

**PAGE 121**
**1.** Q. (They are the initial letters of the first line of the British national anthem.)

**2.** Place coins 1 and 5 on top of coin 3.

**3.** C. (In all the other boxes, the first two figures and the last two figures are squared numbers.)

**PAGE 122**
**4.** 42 ostriches with 84 legs and 40 cows, with 160 legs.

**5.** In triangle A,
1 x 5 x 4 x 8 (from 1548 at the top) = 160 (bottom right). So bottom left = 1 x 6 x 0 = 0.
In triangle B, 3 x 8 x 4 (from 384 at the top) = 96 which should be inserted bottom right. (9 x 6 = 54, which is indeed the figure bottom left.)
In triangle C, 9 x 8 x 7 = 504, which should be inserted bottom right. 5 x 0 x 4 = 0, which should be inserted bottom left.

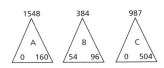

**6.** 9. (8, then 4, then 2, then 1 are subtracted.)

**PAGE 123**
**7.** 80. (The centre is twice the sum of the surrounding petals.)

**8.** 225. (The series 0+1+3+5+7+9 etc is written in a clockwise spiral. They are also the first square numbers.)

**9.** HAILSTONE, SURROGATE, WARMONGER

**PAGE 124**
**10.** He will reach the buoy after 12 hours of rowing on the 14th day. He will then fall asleep and drift downstream for 2km towards the base. On day 15, the current will be with him and he will therefore cover 5km, plus the 2km he drifts while asleep, making a total of 7km. This will leave him 7 km from home – a distance that he will cover on day 16.

**11.**

| 16 | 2 | 3 | 13 |
|----|----|----|----|
| 5 | 11 | 10 | 8 |
| 9 | 7 | 6 | 12 |
| 4 | 14 | 15 | 1 |

**12.** Start at the left part of the tail of the Q on the outer circle, complete the tail up to the right outer circle, go round the circle, then up to the inner left part of the circle and right round.

**PAGE 125**
**13.** 8 + 6 + 7 x 5 = 105

**14.** The lefthand number multiplied by the centre number produces the number directly opposite.

**15.** Meet me at the hideout. (The letters read alternately, from the right, and from the bottom up.)

**PAGE 126**
**16.** 1. (A can be paired with F, B with G, C with D, and E with H.)

**17.** AGINCOURT

**PAGE 127**
**18.** Unused arrow, Al, final arrow B5, first arrow E3.

**19.** A. (The pattern reads the same from any direction.)

SOLUTIONS – SOLUTIONS – SOLUTIONS – SOLUTIONS – SOLUTIONS – SOLUTIONS – SOLUTIONS – SOLUTIONS – SOLUTIONS

**PAGE 128**
**20.** 72. (Numbers on the third figure are the products of their corresponding numbers on the first two.)

**21.** 2. (The lower numbers are one-quarter of the top numbers plus 1.)

**22.** A.

**PAGE 129**
**23.** You could place the three blocks side by side so that they touched each other and remove the middle one. You could then hold the string taut across the gap from A to B where the central block had been.

**24.** B. (The white pointer advances one, three, five, seven etc. letters each time, while the black pointer advances three letters each time.)

**PAGE 130**
**25.**

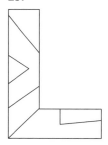

**26.** 1944. (Each balloon is the product of the two balloons immediately below it.)

**27.** The boy makes $1 profit. (60 marbles cost $6, so 3 yo-yos cost $6, which means that 5 yo-yos cost $10. 2 cyberpets therefore cost $10, so 1 costs $5.)

**PAGE 131**
**1.** H. (A can be paired with E, B with I, C with D, and F with G.)

**PAGE 132**
**2.** C. (The white pointer moves forwards nine letters each time, while the black pointer moves backwards four, five, six etc. letters each time.)

**3.** 10.05a.m.

**4.** ONION.

**PAGE 133**
**5.** 26. (The sum of the lefthand petals less the sum of the righthand petals equals the centre in each case.)

**6.**

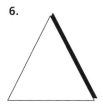

**PAGE 134**
**7.** 36. (The central number in each triangle is twice the sum of the other three.)

**8.**

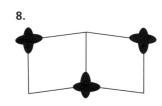

**9.** B. (In all of the others, the sum of the first two digits is equal to the sum of the last two.)

**10.** 13,122. (Each number is half the square of the number below it.)

**PAGE 135**
**11.** 6. (The numbers on the third figure are arrived at by dividing corresponding numbers on the first figure by those on the second figure.)

**12.** K and B. (The letters in the top row increase by one place, then two, then three etc. The lower letters decrease by two, then three, then four etc.

**13.** 27. (The bottom number is four times the top number, minus 5.)

**PAGE 136**
**14.**

**15.** 120. (The series 0 + 1 + 2 + 3 + 4 etc is written in an anticlockwise spiral.)

**16.** Paul is 54, Gillian 81 and Mary, 26.

**PAGE 137**
**17.** 6. ARGENTINA. (The others are
1. ANTELOPE
2. BADGER
3. SPRINGBOK
4. HAMSTER
5. POLECAT.)

**18.** A1

**PAGE 138**
**19.** 54. (It is the sum of all the figures on the platforms below it.)

**20.** ATTENTION, EQUATIONS, TERRAPINS

**21.** LAMBORGHINI

**PAGE 139**
**22.** D

**23.** The sum of the righthand numbers minus the sum of the lefthand numbers gives the centre number.

**24.** 15. (In each instance, the bottom left number is one more than the top, and the bottom right is seven less than the top.)

**PAGE 140**
**25.** 1. (The digits of each of the bottom boxes add up to 8. The digits in each of the boxes in the row above it add up to 4; and those in the third row add up to 2. The sum of each ascending row is thus halved.)

**26.** (9+9)÷.9 = 2
.

**PAGE 141**

1. At the mine that day, Simon placed one ounce of gold in one sack. He then placed one ounce in another sack, which he placed inside the first. He then placed fourteen ounces in the last sack, along with the other two sacks. This meant that the first sack did indeed hold one ounce; the second, two; and the third, sixteen. He had therefore been telling the truth when he gave the witch eight ounces of gold as half of what he had mined that day. But by placing two sacks, with their contents, inside the third sack, it seemed he had lied.

**PAGE 142**

2. F.

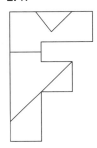

3. 3. (One number is one-third of the largest number, plus the third number.)

4. 23. (The number in the last box of each horizontal row is the sum of the six digits in the first three boxes.)

**PAGE 143**

5. 60. (The central number in each triangle is the product of the other three.)

6. IMPASSIVE, SPINNAKER, THESAURUS

7. T. (D has the same number of straight lines and curves as P, and T has the same number as L.)

**PAGE 144**

8.

| 4 | 6 | 2 | 6 |
|---|---|---|---|
| 2 | 4 | 4 | 8 |
| 5 | 1 | 9 | 3 |
| 7 | 7 | 3 | 1 |

9. S for Saturn. (They are the initial letters of the first six planets, starting with the closest to the Sun – Mercury, Venus, Earth, Mars, Jupiter.)

10. 11. (The pairs of numbers add up to 31 in each alternate case: the others total 32.)

**PAGE 145**

11.

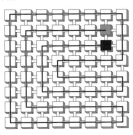

**PAGE 146**

12. 123. (Square each number and add 2 to get the next number.)

13. 5. (The sum total of like shapes is 21.)

14. ROCKY MARCIANO

15. 48. (Consecutive multiplication of the first three numbers in each horizontal row gives the last number – for example, 1x3x4=12.)

**PAGE 147**

16. The centre number is the square root of the sum of any two opposite numbers.

17. 3 melons

18. B

**PAGE 148**

19. D. (The black pointer advances five, six, seven, etc. letters each time, while the white pointer goes back by three, six, nine, twelve, etc, letters each time.)

20. 220. (Work backwards – 33 must be $1/4$ of those left at 4pm. 132 (33 x 4) must therefore be $4/5$ of those left at 3.30pm. 165 (132 ÷ 4 x 5) must therefore be $3/4$ of those left at 3pm. $1/4$ of those left at 3pm is therefore 165 ÷ 3 = 55.
Total number of visitors is therefore 55 x 4 = 220.)

**PAGE 149**

21. C. (From left to right, the black squares are numbers 1, 3, 5, 7 and 9.)

22. Six of Hearts. (Each card is the sum of the two cards directly above it. The suits progress in a zigzag pattern – A, B, C, D, G, F, E, H, I, J.)

**PAGE 150**

23. C. (Only symbols common to the first two shields in each horizontal row appear in the third shield.)

**PAGE 151**

1. ○ = -1, △ = 1, ▢ = 2, B

2. B. (The number of lines to each central shape in each horizontal row is the sum of the sides of each shape on either side.)

**PAGE 152**

3. D. (The white pointer moves two letters forwards, four letters backwards, six letters forwards, eight letters backwards, etc., and the black pointer advances nine letters each time.)

4. The couple did not stipulate that the table or the panels had to be square! It could therefore be shaped exactly as *below*.

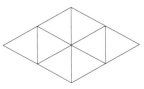

**PAGE 153**

5. 3. (In each flower, the sum of the left-hand petals, divided by the sum of the right-hand petals, equals the centre number.)

6. REALISTIC, ARMISTICE, SKEPTICAL

7. TAGLIATELLE

**PAGE 154**

8. H. (A can be paired with F, B with G, C with E, and D with I.)

**PAGE 155**

9. 26. (From the series 1,2,4,8,16,32 take away the series 1,2,3,4,5 and 6 respectively and place the resulting numbers on each balloon in ascending order.)

**10.**

**11.** Half the sum of the outer circles plus the sum of the inner circles = the figure in the central circle, 53.

**PAGE 156**
**12.** 10 – or 01! (The sum of the individual digits in connecting squares is 12 in every case.)

**13.** 33. (In each triangle, the product of the bottom two numbers plus the top number gives the central number.)

**14.** C - the total number of spots increases in number by two every time.

**PAGE 157**
**15.** The letter is R: reading in a clockwise direction from the segment at the top and skipping every other segment spells out the four seasons of the year: SPRING, SUMMER, AUTUMN and WINTE-R.
**16.** 28. (The top numbers are half the product of the bottom numbers.)

**17.** D. (The bottom two rows repeat the top two rows, in the opposite direction.)

**PAGE 158**
**18.** The central number is the sum of any left-hand number squared plus its opposite number.

**19.** 7. (On each figure, the sum of the round body parts equals the sum of the feet.)

**20.** C

**PAGE 159**
**21.** C

**PAGE 160**
**22.** B. (The black squares are numbers 1, 4 and 9, the first three squared numbers. The fourth grid should therefore have it 16th square filled, 16 being the next squared number, that is 4 x 4.)

**23.** Douglas' son.

**PAGE 161**
**1.** Adele: 3S/10D; Brenda: 2S/3D; Caroline: Ace S/Ace D; Derek: 8D/9D; Evan: 8S/7D; Fred: 4S/4D; Gemma: 9S/10S; Harry: 2D/5D; Isabel: 6S/6D; Jasmine: 5S/7S.

**2.** C

**PAGE 162**
**3.** The trick is to balance the central match of each group of three on top of the other two.

**4.** 5, Comet. (All the others are planets – Neptune, Jupiter, Saturn, Earth, Uranus.)

**PAGE 163**
**5.** I. (Starting from the top bar, multiply 6 x 7 x 1 = 42. Divide by 2 = 21, and take the 21st letter in the alphabet. Then, moving to the next bar in a clockwise direction, multiply 8 x 3 x 2 = 48. Divide by 2 = 24, and take the 24th letter in the alphabet. With the next bar, multiply 6 x 1 x 6 = 36. divide by 2 = 18, and take the 18th letter of the alphabet. Finally, multiply 2 x 3 x 3 = 18. Divide by 2 = 9, and take the 9th letter of the alphabet.)

**6.** Pterosaur, Diplodocus, Triceratops

**PAGE 164**
**7.**

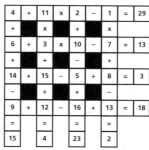

**8.** The Bedhouin who shared his three loaves should have received $1, and the other, $7. (With 8 loaves to share, each of the men would have had 2 2/3 loaves. So the Bedhouin with 3 loaves gave the traveller 1/3 loaf, and the other gave the traveller 2 1/3 loaves, or 7 times as much.)

**PAGE 165**
**9.** D. (A can be paired with E, B with H, C with G, and F with I.)

**PAGE 166**
**10.**

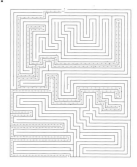

**PAGE 167**
**11.** B5.

**12.** A. (The complete square is rotated 90 degrees clockwise in each instance.)

**13.** MOZAMBIQUE

**PAGE 168**
**14.** 98.
(7 x (3 + 1 + 7 + 3) = 98)

**15.**

| 2 | 17 | 3 | 6 |
|---|----|---|----|
| 2 | 4 | 15 | 7 |
| 17 | 0 | 9 | 2 |
| 7 | 7 | 1 | 13 |

**16.** Four of Hearts. (Each consecutive horizontal row adds up to twice the last. The suits are each represented once per vertical column and alternate red/black in each horizontal row.)

**PAGE 169**

**17.** 48. (The central number is the sum of the individual digits on its surrounding petals.)

**18.** The central number is the sum of the digits in any opposing sectors.

**19.** 4, weighing 1, 3, 9 and 27 pounds respectively. (If, for example, he needed to weigh out 2 pounds of rice, he could put a 1-pound weight on one pan, a 3-pound weight in the other, then add rice to the first pan until one scale balanced the other. Similar methods could be employed for every weight up to 40 pounds.)

**PAGE 170**
**20.**

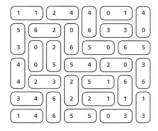

**PAGE 171**
**1.**

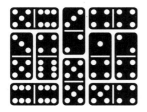

**2.** 0. (Each letter has a position in the alphabet equal to the first digit in each number minus the second.)

**PAGE 172**
**3.** D

**4.** Set your clock at any time – say 3. Go to the village and note the time on the clock there – say 5. Walk back at the same pace. Note the time on your clock now. Divide this by 2, which will give

the time it took you to return – say 20 minutes. The time will therefore be 5.20.

**PAGE 173**
**5.** I've left some cash under the clock for you to buy two papers. Read from the bottom upwards in the 1st column furthest left, and every alternate column after that.

**6.** 4. (Call the coconuts A, B, C and D. Weight A against B, A against C, A against D and B against C. If none of these balance, then you know that C and D must be identical.)

**7.** A. 5 B. 5 C. 7 (Each final figure corresponds to the number of strokes in the preceding Roman numeral.)

**PAGE 174**
**8.** Flat 29A. (The numbers of the flats are the same as the numerical values of the letters in their surnames. The floor letter is one letter previous to the first letter of their names.)

**9.** 4. (Each horizontal row and vertical column adds up to 13.)

| A | I | F | B | E | C | H | G | D |
|---|---|---|---|---|---|---|---|---|
| D | C | H | F | A | G | E | B | I |
| B | G | E | D | H | I | F | A | C |
| H | B | D | C | F | E | G | I | A |
| I | F | C | A | G | D | B | H | E |
| G | E | A | I | B | H | D | C | F |
| E | D | B | G | C | A | I | F | H |
| F | A | I | H | D | B | C | E | G |
| C | H | G | E | I | F | A | D | B |

**PAGE 175**
**10.** Five of Spades. (Each vertical column adds up to nine. The suits progress D, B, A, C, E, G, I, H, F.)

**11.** ROTTWEILER

**PAGE 176**
**12.** FRAMEWORK, FULMINATE, FAVOURITE

**13.** E. (Each lower group of lines – broken/ unbroken – is the opposite of the one above it.)

**PAGE 177**
**14.** A. (In each horizontal row, the third figure is formed from the top of the first and bottom of the second, with colours changed.)

**PAGE 178**
**15.** 1. (Hold up the sequence to a mirror.

**16.** A. 0, B. 1344, C. 3888 (The digits in each bar are multiplied together and the result given in the next bar.)

**PAGE 179**
**17.** 1. (The letters progress from A-F in a repeated zigzag, as shown *below*.)

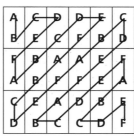

**18.** 5. (The consecutive numbers 2-26 form a clockwise spiral, starting at the centre of the grid.)

**PAGE 180**
**1.** 23. (The product of the first two numbers in any vertical column, minus the third, gives the fourth.)

**2.** Syringe (The others are all parts of the body – throat, stomach, fibula, patella.)

**3.** 1891. (1681 when upside-down.)

**4.** I.

**PAGE 181**
**5.**

19—1—17
2 4 6 8
16—7—14—11—12
3 5 13 15
18—9—10

**6.** B.

**PAGE 182**
**7.** 44. (The sum of the individual digits in the linked circles is 27.)

**8.** B. (The white pointer advances by seven, six, five and four letters, while the black pointer goes back eight places, forwards four places, back two places and forwards one place.)

**PAGE 183**
**9.** 32,547,891 x 6 = 195,287,346

**10.** Exhilerate, starry, northern, fraught. (Each word contains two adjacent letters that are consecutive in the order in which they occur in alphabet.)

**11.** Janice, 22 and 25; Irene, 24 and 27; Mandy, 21 and 23; Clive, 28 and 29; Daryl, 20 and 26.

**PAGE 184**
**12.** 3 & C

**13.** 1152. (Each number is half the product of the previous two.)

## :: LEVEL 20 ::

**PAGE 185**
**14. (**You must always start in room 9 and finish in chamber d. This is because they are the only rooms to have an odd number of doorways, and you cannot go in and out of any place, using each door once only, if it has an odd number of doors. However, by starting in room 9 and finishing in chamber d, each of the doors is used only once.)

**PAGE 186**
**15.**

| 6 | 0 | 5 | 2 | 4 | 3 |
|---|---|---|---|---|---|
| 1 | 6 | 3 | 4 | 0 | 2 |
| 4 | 1 | 6 | 0 | 3 | 5 |
| 3 | 2 | 4 | 5 | 1 | 6 |
| 0 | 3 | 1 | 6 | 2 | 4 |
| 5 | 4 | 0 | 3 | 6 | 1 |

**PAGE 187**
**16.** Three of hearts. (Every horizontal row adds up to eight. The suits progress A, C, F, H, I, G, D, B, E.)

**17.** R.

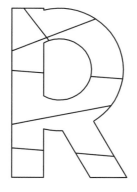

**PAGE 188**
**1.**

**UP**:
**19** Mr Small, **17** Mrs Jay, **16** Ms Benson, **13** Mr Knight,
**11** Miss Allen, **8** Bobby Sims, **7** Mrs Sims, **5** Mr Fraser,
**3** Mrs Cox, **2** Mr Cox.

**DOWN**:
**1** Mr Lee, **3** Mr Donaldson, **4** Mr Philips, **7** Mr Rowe,
**8** Mrs Rowe, **10** Miss Oliver, **13** Ms Wells, **15** Mr Chalfont, **17** Mrs Vernon,
**18** Sally Vernon.

**PAGE 189**
**2.** 9. (The last row is the sum of the first three – that is, 1545+3780+2634 = 7959.)

**3.** DECOUPAGE, MOTORCADE, SECONDARY

**4.** That that is, is: that that is not, is not. That that is, is not that that is not: that that is not, is not that that is. Is not that it? It is!

**PAGE 190**
**5.** You need to proceed as follows:

| Start | B | R | G | B | R | G | B | R | G | | |
|---|---|---|---|---|---|---|---|---|---|---|---|
| 1 | B | R | G | B | R | | | R | G | G | B |
| 2 | | | G | B | R | B | R | R | G | G | B |
| 3 | G | G | G | B | R | B | R | R | | | B |
| 4 | G | G | G | B | | | R | R | R | B | B |
| 5 | G | G | G | B | B | B | R | R | R | | |

**PAGE 191**
**6.** Splendid, fabulous

**7.** BED, HOCK, HEX, DECK, COD

**PAGE 192**
**8.** 1 & H

**9.** In each word, the letters are in alphabetical order.

**PAGE 193**
**10.** The sum of the corner blocks, minus the sum of the intermediate blocks, equals the central block.

**11.** 68 books.

**PAGE 194**
**12.** Well done!
You have worked your way through hundreds of puzzles. You deserve a rest! (The code is based on the following grid shape. The second letter in each section always has a dot within its shape; a third within that section or an identically-shaped section, 2 dots; a fourth, 3 dots.)

| AB | CD | EF |
|---|---|---|
| GH | IJ | KL |
| MN | OP | QR |
| ST | UV | WXYZ |